A
*L*IVELY
ORACLE

A
*L*IVELY
ORACLE

A Centennial Celebration of
P.L. TRAVERS,
Creator of Mary Poppins

Ellen Dooling Draper and
Jenny Koralek, Editors

Published for the Paul Brunton Philosophic Foundation by
LARSON PUBLICATIONS

Cover image by William M. Benson

International Standard Book Number: 0-943924-94-9
Library of Congress Catalog Card Number: 99-73732

Published for the Paul Brunton Philosophic Foundation by
Larson Publications
4936 NYS Route 414, Burdett, New York 14818 USA

05 04 03 02 01 00 99

10 9 8 7 6 5 4 3 2 1

Photographs of P.L. Travers on pages 2 and 100 are reprinted through the courtesy of Patricia L Feltham.
Photographs of P.L. Travers on pages 16 and 210 are reprinted by arrangement with the Mitchell Library, State Library of New South Wales, Sydney, Australia.

The Editors would like to thank
Bernard Courtenay-Mayers, Patricia Feltham,
Lorraine Kisly, Jacqueline Korn (of David Higham Associates),
and Brian Sibley for their generous help
with the preparation of this book.

CONTENTS

Contents

INTRODUCTION

by Ellen Dooling Draper

J UST AS A SEEKER OF TREASURE, on turning up a spadeful of ore, shines a lantern on individual nuggets to discover what answering light might shoot forth from each stone, so P.L. Travers shone the light of her questioning on the characters and themes of each story as she mined the lode of myth. Over the more than fifty years of her delving, she invited us to look with her into the stories and fables of the world, from Australian creation myths to Celtic tales to Navajo legends to the epics of India. The elements that reemerged from these great sources took on new energy and found new form in her books, in the articles she wrote for magazines and newspapers, in the texts of her lectures, and in countless interviews.

At the time of her death in April 1996, readers of *Parabola, The Magazine of Myth and Tradition,* and those who had read the collected essays in *What the Bee Knows* (Penguin, 1993) were well acquainted with the width and breadth of P.L. Travers' writing in the field of mythology. But for the general public, she is remembered only as the creator of Mary Poppins. Three other books she wrote which have not yet received the recognition they deserve are *Friend Monkey, The Fox at the Manger,* and *About the Sleeping Beauty.*

The aim of the present volume is to shine light on *all* of P.L. Travers' work. Out of respect for her privacy, Part One, Biographical Notes, is brief, giving information about her long life that she herself had

9

willingly shared with her friends and readers. Part Two is devoted to *Mary Poppins*—the series of books and the Disney movie. Part Three examines her other books, *About the Sleeping Beauty, Friend Monkey,* and *The Fox at the Manger.* Part Four focuses on the underlying themes that ran through all of her writing, and Part Five includes transcripts and impressions of her spoken words. In Part Six we are reprinting three important articles by P.L. Travers which are not available elsewhere. The contributors to this collection of essays are all writers and editors who knew her personally or professionally. In rereading what she has written and said, we have rediscovered P.L. Travers' keen mind and abundant spirit and deepened our enormous sense of gratitude for the many times she has opened our minds to the lessons of myth.

Like an echo of the great mythological truths that informed her writing, the call of what lies *beyond* sounds throughout P.L. Travers' work. We reach the last page, close the book, and hear the invitation to keep going. With neither a conclusion nor a looking back, each story is as boundless as the journey of the swan:

> A long way and yet no distance. The end of the world is hard to find, but it may be as near as it is far, east of the sun and west of the moon or just around the corner. (*The Fox at the Manger*)

Sometimes, the story's last words open new vistas upward and outward:

> And high above them the great shape circled and wheeled through the darkening sky, shining and keeping its secret for ever and ever and ever . . . (*Mary Poppins Comes Back*)

At other times, within the context of our most familiar surroundings, the story ends with a promise:

> The morning air was bright and clear, the birds were singing their autumn songs, and the Park Keeper was coming towards them with a late rose stuck in his cap . . . (*Mary Poppins in the Park*)

P.L. Travers herself was always ready for more. While recuperating from a broken shoulder in 1993, she read Natalie Baan's retelling of "The Seven Swans" in *Parabola*'s issue on "Healing" and was reminded of an old question. "I have always wondered," she said, "how the seventh brother's story went on. What must it have been like, to pass the rest of his days with a wing instead of an arm?" But the question remained unanswered, because even with the availability of modern technology—"Please, tell us what happened to him! You could speak it into a tape recorder, and someone could write it down for you . . ." —she could not bear the idea of putting her thoughts into a mechanical device. For her, writing was always done with a blue-inked fountain pen or a faint-ribboned manual typewriter (originals which, as all her editors well know, produced barely legible gray on gray photocopies). And by the time she recovered from the broken shoulder, the ravages of arthritis and the growing weakness of extreme old age made it impossible for her to write again. So the question of what happened to the seventh brother after the story's "Happy Ever After" is one we will have to ponder on our own.

What lies beyond in terms of time and space was another question P.L. Travers explored. Through a door left enticingly ajar, she gives us many peeks of other realities where the rules are different. In the wink of an eye, we step into a painting or a miniature world or, suddenly freed from the law of gravity, we float on the ceiling; another wink, and we are back where we started—somewhat out of breath.

Beyond that partly open door, the unique ones—Mary Poppins, "the Oddity . . . the Great Exception," or Professor McWhirter, "the One and Only" (*Friend Monkey*)—clearly are at home and at ease. On this side of the door, the everyday realities depicted by Travers (sun-dappled parks where nannies push perambulators, or teatime with linen napkins) may not be exactly familiar to us today; nevertheless, the glimpses of the truly unusual on the other side of the doorway still stand apart and call to our imagination. We read on, now expecting the unexpected, and notice that the boundaries between the known and unknown seem to shift and shimmer.

> "Is it his dinner time?" asked Michael.
> "Well—no!" said a little scratchy voice. "As a matter of fact, it's breakfast!"
> "How clever Jane is!" thought Michael admiringly. "She can not only make a little old man, she can talk like one as well."
> But her eyes, as he met them, were full of questions.

"Did you speak, Michael, in that squeaky way?
"Of course he didn't," said the voice again.

And now it is time for us to step across the sill. But we do not have to be afraid, because P.L. Travers herself is there "in between"—between here and there, past and present, "the end" and "the afterward"—to give us a helping hand across the threshold. She stands in the place where story lives.

Travers tells us that stories are not invented or made up. Rather, they spring eternally from a source common to all places and times, finding new expression through the writer. "The best you can do," she tells us in "I Never Wrote for Children," "is to be there to jot them down." She appreciated the generosity of such stories and their accessibility to everyone; she never understood why booksellers insisted on categorizing the audience, for instance, as "Adult," or "Children 8–10." She wrote stories because they were there to be "jotted down." If they were enjoyed by the very young or by the very old, she was equally pleased. Her open-mindedness in this regard probably stemmed from the fact that as a young child she had read whatever books she could get her hands on—Lewis Carroll, Beatrix Potter, Dickens, Sir Walter Scott, the Bible, technical farming journals—all with the same enthusiasm.

And then there were the "stories told"—Irish legends and Grimm's fairy tales—which she heard from her parents and from Matilda, the woman who came in to do the washing. Travers' young soul was deeply etched with impressions of the cadences and rhythms, the multi-layered realities, and the magic and heroism of the tales. These impressions kindled the questions that occupied her for the rest of her life.

Interviewers over the years asked Travers where she got the idea for Mary Poppins, and she always insisted that she had *discovered* Mary Poppins, not *invented* her. And she always seemed surprised when people did not perceive Mary Poppins as she herself did—as if she expected everyone to get to know the magical nanny simply by following her and listening to her as she makes her way through the various stories. Travers' responses to the preliminary drafts of the screenplay produced at Disney's studio were eloquent, with occasional undertones of indignation, as she instructed the writers about how to portray Mary Poppins:

> The humor, the absurdity, and the pathos, comes from the fact that she is, indeed, like a Dutch doll, not pretty in the least, and it is this that makes her vanity so funny.
>
> It is Mary Poppins' plainness of person, her absolute rightness, without ever being pert, her calm and serene behavior in the midst of the most unlikely adventures that make the fun of the story. If her gravity is not maintained, all the point is lost. She is always feminine, prim, neat, demure, sniffy, arrogant, but always keeps within her own frame.
>
> There was no love affair between her and Bert, it is quite impossible that Mary Poppins should be in love with any mortal.
>
> She would never say "Don't you think?" She states, she does not ask for anyone's opinion. And, by the way, she doesn't speak Cockney. She has the most demure, unaccented voice.

In playing the title role in the movie, Julie Andrews came to know the character she was playing, and since then, to appreciate why Mary Poppins remains so universally appealing.

> I have always been curious as to why audiences have embraced Mary Poppins over the years, because at first glance one might think this lady was overly strict and old-fashioned.
>
> Perhaps her popularity reflects, not just a desire for her ability to make magic, but for something often more difficult to achieve: loving, safe boundaries—with a lot of fun thrown in.

The ongoing friction between what she knew and no one else yet understood about the characters and scenes in her books was also an important element in relation to the illustrations. Prior to the publication of the original *Mary Poppins,* Travers needed to find an illustrator. This process began one day when she was visiting a friend and saw a hand-drawn Christmas card featuring a mounted knight carrying a banner. She was so captivated by the horse's hoof-prints that she immediately demanded to know who the artist was, and this was how she met Mary Shepard.

A decades-long collaboration between the two women followed. From the beginning, Travers sought to convey to Shepard the spirit of the book's central character and of those who peopled the neighborhood of Cherry Tree Lane and the Park. Author and artist went for walks together through Hyde Park, stopping to observe children who resembled Michael and Jane, watching the way they moved or sat still. Travers gave Shepard a wooden Dutch doll to serve as model for Mary Poppins, and told her about the books' timelessness and how the characters were not to get older from one book to the next.

Over the next fifty-four years, from the time that *Mary Poppins* first appeared in 1934 until the last time she bid the children good-night in 1988, Travers maintained a close working relationship with Shepard, often criticizing and occasionally praising her drawings. The result is that the images, which usually catch the characters in the middle of a motion which begs to be followed, succeed in drawing the reader directly into the story. And today, Shepard's image of Mary Poppins borne aloft on her umbrella is recognized all over the world. A recent *New York Times* article about home care for children in the United States employed the figure as the symbol for "nanny."

Since Travers' death, many people have asked for more details about her private life. But she, like Mary Poppins, always maintained an aura of the unknown about her that made the uncovering of "personal details" virtually impossible. No one knew where either one of them went "on their days off." Travers was adamant in guarding her private life. She refused to answer any questions of a personal nature—sometimes with such a degree of curmudgeonliness that she came to be anything but a sought-after assignment by certain journalists. She even left explicit instructions in her will that there were to be no biographies written about her.

Therefore, out of the respect we all bore her, the editors and contributors to this book have honored her wishes in this regard. Those biographical details that Travers herself spoke or wrote about can be found in two pieces: "Refining Nectar" by Ben Haggarty (which he composed with Travers' blessing during her last months and delivered as the eulogy at her funeral on May 1, 1996) and "Ever Afterwards," an obituary written for *The Guardian* by Adrian House, Travers' one-time editor and long time friend.

To complete the portrait, our book ends with a respectful personal view, entitled "P.L. Travers from A to Z." This piece echoes one of three small books by Travers that are not covered in this present volume but merit rediscovery. On the surface, Travers' book was a straightforward ABC book for children, underneath whose simple exterior lie many lessons about myth and story. Koralek's "A to Z," while respecting her cherished privacy, contains many insights into Travers' writing soul.

We invite you on a journey of discovery—one of the most compelling themes in the writing of P. L. Travers. The sense of the journey, particularly the search for the road leading back home, was perhaps one of her father's strongest legacies to her (even though he died when she was a very young child). His nostalgia for Ireland was such a powerful influence on her youth that as soon as she was old enough, she left Australia and returned to Ireland, as it were, in his stead. As she got older, the sense of being far from home (while at the same time feeling very much at home "in this most beautiful world") drew her more and more urgently to find that special place where opposites meet, the place where fairy tales end. And she invited us to accompany her.

We dedicate our efforts in this book to the work of P. L. Travers and to her unrelenting quest, her hearkening to the call of that distant but perhaps not completely inaccessible "Happy Ever After."

PART ONE

BIOGRAPHICAL NOTES

REFINING NECTAR

by Ben Haggarty

P AMELA TRAVERS was born in the Australian outback in the penultimate year of the nineteenth century, "caught," as she said, "between the horns of an Irish father and a mother of Scottish and Irish descent."[1] There she and her two younger sisters had an upbringing which she called "traditional," marked by a rugged simplicity. Everyone worked hard when hard work was called for and made entertainment at home— through stories, music, song, and dance—when the time could be afforded, or occasion demanded it. There were books in the house: a basic collection of classics, some Irish poetry, and two red volumes of the Grimm's Tales.

She refers a great deal to her parents in her writing because "parents are a child's first gods and responsible, whether they know it or not, for many seeds of fate."[2] In 1910, the children were woken in the middle of the night by their mother to see Halley's comet—an experience which made a profound impression on Pamela. It merged with a memory of her father's favorite oath "By the Lord Harry!" to become "Harry's comet"—a symbol of a remote and fiery-tailed God, far away yet destined to return again and again. Her father had died three years before and the loss of his rich presence marked her deeply. "I remember his melancholy, which was the other side of his Irish gaiety, and know it was catching and inheritable."[3]

From an early age she exhibited her bold spirit. Because her father had often spoken wistfully of "home," that "most distressful country," she, who sometimes saw herself as a boy, yearned to buy the 19/11d Air Gun advertised on the back of a "Buffalo Bill" penny book (which claimed it could kill an elephant at five yards). She had no doubts that she would then "slay the enemies of Ireland."[4]

"So much depends of the quality of Grown ups," she wrote later in an essay about education.[5] The important "Grown ups" of her childhood were "a trinity known as Father, Mother, and Mat." Matilda was an Irish washerwoman who endlessly told the children "grims"—a word the young Pamela took to be a generic term for narrative. Mat sowed a seed.

Pamela's impression of the Australian bush perfectly evokes the palpable presence of the mythic dimension which had so strongly influenced her as a child:

> By night you went about cautiously lest the Pleiades catch in your hair. . . . All was present and immediate, everything whole and complete, not a thing was missing.[6]

Here, she would stand for hours, "listening to silence."

> Be still long enough, I thought, and the trees would take no notice of me and continue whatever it was they were doing or saying before I happened upon them. For nothing was more certain, to my mind, than that they lived a busy and communicative life which ceased—as at a command given—whenever I appeared.[7]

After a period as a dancer and actress in a traveling theater company (to which she referred with glee in later years), she crossed the ocean in her early twenties, to arrive in Dublin. There, the Celtic Twilight, which had "cast its long blue light" over her childhood, "had practically turned into night." But she "caught it by the tail."[8] She met the writer and artist A.E. (George Russell) "whose thought was crystal clear and hard—and still had room for Dryads."[9] He became her great mentor, a second father. Through him she met Yeats, Padraic Colum, James Stephens, Lady Gregory, Bernard Shaw and a host of other spirits—all of whom "cheerfully licked [her] into shape like a set of mother cats with a kitten."[10] A Dublin uncle didn't like her "gallivanting around with men who see fairies."[11] But such disapproval only redoubled her enthusiasm and, with AE's whole-hearted encouragement, she continued to produce articles and poetry for publication in *The Irish Statesman*.

The aftermath of "The Great War" witnessed an intense and urgent interest in questions of metaphysics and spirituality. Yeats was translating the Upanishads, and, through AE, Pamela was introduced in England to A.R. Orage, who published her work in *The New English Weekly*. That was the beginning of a path which led her to C.S. Nott, P.D. Ouspensky, and G.I. Gurdjieff.

All this fertilized the ground onto which Mary Poppins dropped in 1933, borne fully formed by the East Wind. She was "The Great Exception"[12]—the only one who didn't forget—who could remember the language of the trees, the sunlight and the stars.

She wrote two other children's novels, *Friend Monkey* and *I Go by Sea, I Go by Land,* as well as the haunting Christmas meditation *The Fox at the Manger.* However, the legacy of her writing for adults is what now deserves a wider public acknowledgement than it received during her lifetime.

Throughout her life she wrote and spoke publicly about the creative process—most famously in her 1966 address to the Library of Congress, titled, after E.M. Forster, "Only Connect." In this she mapped out many of the concerns that would occupy her over the next thirty years, including Myth, Fairy Tale, and the Metaphysics of the Nursery Rhyme; The Aboriginal Dreaming; Zen; Woman and Her Role in Life; and the Proximity of the Mythic to the Everyday.

In 1976, in New York, her friend D.M. Dooling (at the age of sixty-six) began a new venture—*Parabola, The Magazine of Myth and Tradition.* This quarterly journal took a theme for each issue which, under Mrs. Dooling's firm editorial direction, was activated by questioning.

Pamela at seventy-seven had a lifetime of rich experiences behind her. She had listened to the silence of the bush, played Shakespearean roles in the outback, crossed the world to plunge barefoot though Irish bogs, brought the cosmos into Cherry Tree Lane, received a secret name from Navajo elders, dined at the table of G.I. Gurdjieff, raked gardens of sand in Japan . . . She now found in *Parabola* the medium in which all that experience could be brought together, in response to great themes such as The Witness, Repetition and Renewal, Death, The Trickster, Sacrifice and Transformation. Through this writing she would leave a fine nectar to feed us—"the Grown Ups"—the ones responsible for the education of future generations.

Her first essay in *Parabola,* on "The World of the Hero," changed my life. I had just finished school and was confronted fair and square with a challenge and a set of questions that had never been put to me before:

> Everybody has to be the hero of one story: his own. . . . Not to be the hero of one's own story—could one agree to that?[13]

Whenever *Parabola* arrived, I would read Mrs. Dooling's "Focus," and then immediately turn to Pamela's piece. It was always surprising, full of stars yet absolutely grounded—her hair was never caught in the Pleiades—as she ranged freely through the mythologies of the world, setting up true resonances between diverse cultures and traditions, always finding an appropriate place from which to ponder an image or situation.

Pamela's public talks and lectures during the 1970s and 80s had an audacious charm. She played freely not only with ideas and symbols but with her audiences as well. I'll never forget her coaxing two hundred reserved English adults into singing, with great abandon and joy, the nursery rhymes they had probably not sung since childhood.

For her, creativity and life merged in the phrase "thinking is linking." This didn't mean indulging in random association but, rather, linking attention in a special way with a consciousness that she likened to both the Aboriginal Dreaming and the Celtic Cauldron. When we confided our thoughts to her, she would say "put them in your cauldron—and *never* conclude!"

> The cauldron of plenty in each of us seethes with its ferment, sweet and bitter—the world to be carried and no plaint made; love to suffer long and be kind, not vaunting, not puffed up; the seed that we carry to be threshed, freed from its crusty husk; the aching question of who we are and for what made, answered only by its echo; the need to stand before the unknown and never ask to know; to take our leave of the world, head high, no matter how hard the parting . . .[14]

That was Pamela's way. That was the way she tried.

For many, many years Pamela lived in preparation for death. As she finally approached, barefoot, the flower-shaped central stone (known variously as Ciel, Jerusalem, The Holy City, and la Mort) of the Maze at Chartres, she came to the following:

> Well, Death, what have I to bring you? Only this—my burden! And, as well, certain scraps of meaning. For, if my life happened to me, there have been moments—may they be counted—when I have happened to it. . . . Let me not, therefore, be a Sabine woman, part of your plunder, borne off in protest. I would encounter darkness as a bride and eat of the pomegranate![15]

She wrote her own obituary in the *Parabola* issue on "Memory and Forgetting," in a piece called "Lively Oracles." It is an ecstatic dialogue with Taliesin, whom she calls the "Soul's Remembrancer," and it ends in this way:

> A Dieu, Taliesin, Bard of Elphin! Where the center holds and the end folds into the beginning there is no such word as fare-well. . . .
>
> My shadow follows me as I walk westward. The sunset spreads it along the grass, taller and lordlier, now, than I. What will be remembered in it, this changing incorporeal shape—compact of myself and the sun? When the tides of evening come flowing in we shall both be lost to sight. May the Lord have mercy on me and my shadow.[16]

And so we return to silence, the silence that she listened to as a child in the bush. The silent way of being that she admired so much in the Navajo people. The silence of linking, of connecting. The fine, vibrating, light yet deep silence to which she listened for so long, so consistently and so carefully. Which spoke through her. And which she has now become.

NOTES

1. "Only Connect," *What the Bee Knows*, p. 286. (First published in *Quarterly Journal of Library of Congress*, 1967.)

2. "A Radical Innocence," *What the Bee Knows: Reflections on Myth, Symbol and Story.* London and New York: Penguin, 1993. p. 239. (First published in *The New York Times*, 1965.)

3. *Ibid.*

4. "Only Connect," p. 287.

5. "A Radical Innocence," p. 236.

6. "Now Farewell and Hail," *What the Bee Knows*, p. 166. (First published in *Parabola*, "The Child," 1979.)

7. "The Death of A.E.: Irish Hero and Mystic," *What the Bee Knows*, p. 242. (First published in *The Celtic Consciousness*, ed. Prof. R. O'Driscoll. New York: Braziller, 1981.)

8. *Ibid.*, p. 242.

9. "Only Connect," p. 293.

10. *Ibid.*, p. 290.

11. *Ibid.*, p. 291.

12. *Mary Poppins*, "John and Barbara's Story."

13. "The World of the Hero," *What the Bee Knows*, p. 17. (First published in *Parabola*, "The Hero," 1976.)

14. "Zen Moments: *Sunt Lachymae Rerum*," *What the Bee Knows*, p. 202. (First published in *Parabola*, "A Sense of Humor," 1987.)

15. "Walking the Maze at Chartres," *What the Bee Knows*, p. 136. (First published in *Parabola*, "Guilt," 1983.)

16. "Lively Oracles," *What the Bee Knows*, p. 188. (First published in *Parabola*, "Memory and Forgetting," 1986.)

EVER AFTERWARDS

by Adrian House

To SURVIVE the impact of later life as lovers and mothers, sales-
men and nurses, soldiers and judges, children need regular
inoculations of magic and alarm. To survive the impact of their children, wise parents provide these injections by reading to them aloud.
Which is why a multitude of children, parents, and grandparents all over
the world are so grateful to P.L. Travers. Her myths enchanted them for
more than sixty years—ever since her most famous creation, Mary
Poppins, a unique and unnerving children's nanny, first parachuted into
the life of a family *she* chose, on her colored umbrella with its talking
parrot-head handle. She is probably looking down, with a glint in her
superior blue eye, confident that she will be around for a great deal
longer than her maker's four score years and sixteen, for she has become
a classic. Like all classics she emerged from an imagination touched by
genius, but neither author nor character are easy to trace to their
sources.

The author first. At the turn of the century, a daughter Helen Lyndon
was born to an Irish rancher in Queensland, Robert Travers Goff. She
was seven when he died. At eleven she was sent to a boarding school
equipped, she wrote, with a God who had a son but no wife, and therefore must cook for himself; a love of the night sky glittering with the
constellations that frequent her books; and a handguide of "simple tribal

25

cryptograms," essential to the understanding of life, encoded in Grimm's Fairy Tales.

She started work as a journalist in Sydney, but when she went on the stage to dance and act Shakespeare, she picked a new name, Pamela Lyndon Travers. She used that name when her first poem was printed by a newspaper editor called Murdoch (he later had a son called Rupert). Moving to London she wrote articles, poems, and reviews for *The New English Weekly*. A poem she sent to *The Irish Statesman* led to a friendship with its editor, the poet/painter/economist AE, who became as close as or closer than the father she had lost.

Early in the 1930s Mary Poppins flew into her head, and no sooner were the first two or three stories on paper than they were eagerly seized by the publisher Peter Davies. *Mary Poppins* made her debut in 1934, followed by two sequels in 1935 and 1944. The three books were immediate best-sellers.

When war broke out in 1939, Pamela worked for a time in the Ministry of Information. Later she adopted and brought up a son. After the war she was backed by an energetic new publisher, William Collins, who lent her an attic in his office to encourage her to start writing again. His energetic promotion and distribution of her books helped her reap the rewards when Walt Disney's film carried Mary Poppins to parts of the planet her umbrella could not reach. Although Pamela relished the phenomenal success of the film and was delighted by Julie Andrews as her heroine, she could not abide the spoonfuls of sugar with which her work had been coated. Astringence was an essential ingredient of her character.

Her last thirty years were devoted to a quest for meaning in life. She searched among the Navajo in America, through Japan's world of Zen, in Jung's footsteps in Switzerland, and on her knees as a Christian. Her hunt produced a number of books: *The Fox at the Manger* (1962), *Friend Monkey* (1971), and *About the Sleeping Beauty* (1975). After a succession of occasional pieces on symbolism, psychology, and allegory appeared in *Parabola* Magazine, they were collected in *What the Bee Knows* (1988).

There was never any question that P.L. Travers possessed a sharp mind and warm heart. From her asides on Leda and the Swan, Sleeping Beauty's pricked finger, and "the erotic thrill" of stealing apples as a child, it is obvious that she was equally alive to her senses. Friendships she knew; she cared deeply for her son, his wife, and their children; she received an honorary doctorate from Chatham College, Pittsburgh, an OBE from the Queen, and a fortune in royalties (with some of which she endowed an award). Nevertheless in an essay on sadness she hints at a longing, perhaps for love, that was never fulfilled.

I have always felt, perhaps wrongly, that there were two phases of her life which were profoundly significant to her, but about which she was always reticent. Although we skirted round their edges, she never discussed them. The first was the period of her friendship with A.E. in Ireland; the second, the war years and the adoption of her son.

I sensed that whatever she had experienced then, the sun shone a little less brightly afterwards, and that if she had been able to control events as she could the contents of her chapters, she would have composed them rather differently. Yet she never lost the warmth of her sympathies and interest in others, young or old. Asked for her opinions or advice she would brood, and then deliver them with intelligence, wisdom, and humor.

I remember her meeting the gaze of a month-old baby and predicting—accurately—the sorrows or joys waiting just round the corner for him. And it was she who suggested that the painter Cecil Collins and his work would perfectly illustrate the theme of the television series *Art, Faith and Vision*. They did, and a remarkable program about Collins was completed a month before he died.

And the origin of Mary Poppins. All her life Pamela evaded the persistent question, "How did you invent Mary Poppins?" If her genesis was spontaneous the question could not be answered, but in 1988 a mist in her mind partially lifted. One night, after Pamela's father died, her mother left her, aged ten, alone with her two little sisters—on a night of thunder, lightning, and torrential rain—to drown herself in a creek. Suddenly Pamela was aware that she possessed a gift, a spell strong enough to confound nightmare. Huddling her sisters under an eiderdown in front of the fire, she started to tell them a story about a small horse. The spell worked until her bedraggled mother returned. The nightmare was over, but Pamela's gift never left her. Happily it has continued to delight her, and us, ever afterwards.

Originally published in *The Guardian*, April 25, 1996

PART TWO

MARY POPPINS

WORLDS BEYOND WORLDS

A Glimpse into the Mary Poppins Books

by Jenny Koralek

"There are worlds beyond worlds and times beyond times, all of them true, all of them real, and all, as children know, penetrating each other."

—P.L. Travers

E VERYONE SEEMS to have heard of Mary Poppins. Her name has passed into folk memory and is often used and abused to represent some kind of longed-for, preferably pretty super-nanny to take complete charge and keep everything shipshape and under control. One can even detect a faint, wistful hope that there will be some magic about her: a discreet sliding up of banisters, a raised finger and in a trice the washing up will be done, the dirty clothes picked up off the floor, the children bathed and in bed, rosy, damp, angelic.

For this attractive but ultimately shallow imprint, we have to thank the Walt Disney film, released to universal delight in 1964: a squeaky clean Mary Poppins played by Julie Andrews; wide-eyed Jane and Michael played by unaffected English children with high, sweet voices; the inimitably husky and breathless Glynis Johns as a charming, giddy Mrs. Banks (but a *suffragette?*—totally out of keeping with the Mrs. Banks of the books);—and the great David Tomlinson marvelously suitable as the good but tetchy father, Mr. Banks.

Of course, there is also Dick van Dyke as Bert, the pavement artist and Chimney Sweep. His grasp of these respectful, loving, and conniving relationships to Mary Poppins is beguiling; but it is utterly ruined whenever he opens his mouth to let forth his execrable Cockney (an accent so elusive to American actors).

Sure, in the film, when Mary Poppins steps into his picture, he gets to take her on a magical Day Out. And yes, the Bird Woman is there on the steps of a Hitchcockian rendering of St. Paul's Cathedral, feeding the birds "tuppence a bag." There is magic in the medicines, and Mary Poppins does slide up the banister. And the opening shots of the East Wind getting up and her arrival at the gate do give one shivers of happy anticipation.

The great set piece, "Chim Chiminee," where hundreds of sweeps leap about on the rooftops of London, belongs in that truly great modern tradition unique to the USA—the musical with infinitely hummable tunes and tap-dancing routines that set us dreaming we have the feet of Gene Kelly or Fred Astaire, and which one would be mealy-mouthed indeed not to thoroughly enjoy and even wholeheartedly relish.

There are also brief exchanges of dialogue which we can be certain came from the author's pen. They touch us and leave us vaguely aware of some other, deeper level in this story trying to make itself heard above the din. "Is that in the book?" adults ask. Getting an answer in the affirmative, they have been heard to murmur, "Hmmm . . ." distinctly meaning, "Ah, well, *now* I understand why you read more than the one promised chapter to the children at bed-time."

BUT . . .

Where are the Twins, John and Barbara, baby Annabel and the Starling? Where is Robertson Aye? Mrs. Brill, and Ellen? Where is the Policeman, Egbert, the triplets? And Herbert and Albert, his brothers, who went off to "*distant lands to mix with giraffes and leopards*"? And Admiral Boom and Binnacle? Miss Lark, the dog-lover? Why no sign of the darker side of these stories? Where is that "*Holy Terror,*" Miss Andrew, Mr. Banks' Governess, who can still turn his legs to jelly (a sinister figure, unreformed to the bitter end, with her caged bird and her equally caged brown-skinned servant boy)? What about The Prime

Minister, the absent-minded Professor, Mrs. Corry and Annie and Fannie? Nellie Rubina and poor old Uncle Dodger, and Florimund and Veritain and little Amor? What's happened to Neleus, the marble boy, and Maia of the Pleiades? And the Red Cow looking for her lost star?

Where are the magic outings, sometimes at night, sometimes during the day, where the familiar world is always turned on its head?

Where is the flying and the dancing?

Where is the Park and, above all, *where is that constant irritant and source of friction, the Park Keeper?*

What substance, and how much of the four books which could have been drawn on, are missing from that video we take out from time to time for our children or our grandchildren? Where is the voice of the author, P.L. Travers, faithfully transmitting the effects of the authentic Mary Poppins on that family at Number Seventeen Cherry Tree Lane? Where but in the books, read long ago—or never read.

There are six of them: *Mary Poppins* (1934), *Mary Poppins Comes Back* (1935), *Mary Poppins Opens the Door* (1944), *Mary Poppins in the Park* (1952), *Mary Poppins in Cherry Tree Lane* (1982), *Mary Poppins and the House Next Door* (1988). There is also the enchanting alphabetic addendum to the first four books, *Mary Poppins from A–Z* (1963); a collection of Mary Poppins' favorite nursery recipes; and a coloring book. This substantial oeuvre contains material of quite cosmic proportions which deserves to be studied closely. (Such a content, thank God, is not unheard of in children's literature; particularly Anglo-Saxon children's literature, but it is nevertheless rare enough to warrant acknowledgement and appreciation).

There are flaws of course. The setting may seem to adult eyes dated, fly-in-amber, stuck in a time-warp, permanently fixed somewhere between the two World Wars; but it is as consistent as Mary Poppins herself. Children find no fault with such things in many of their other favorite serial books, such as *Pippi Longstocking, The Little House on The Prairie,* or the resurgent *Anne of Green Gables.* The author could be accused of social snobbery: The books are a perfect module of the entire English class system, with everyone in their place and knowing it.

The more serious charge of racism was laid at Travers' door in the

1970s by Californian librarians, and caused her great distress. But allowances should surely be made for her conditioning. The British Empire and all that went with it at its glorious zenith was the greatest outer influence on everyone of her time, class, and background—particularly in the northeastern corner of Australia where she was raised.

Young children, apparently, do not perceive such problems in her work. They don't seem to react or project the way adults do. They seem quite able to take it all on board: accepting accents and ways of talking and behaving for just what they are, with no socio-political implications or hidden agendas.

The author was thirty-five when the first book was published in 1934, and eighty-seven when the last was published in 1988—a span of fifty-two years of a very long life. (She was to over-run the traditional "three score years and ten" by twenty-seven years!) This life-span is, on close study, reflected in the books. They are not sequels in the ordinary sense, but develop and deepen as the author's life-story developed and her soul-story deepened.

After the initial energetic impulse which produced two books within one year, about ten years elapsed between the second and the third book; ten again between the third and fourth, *thirty* between the fourth and the fifth, and a mere six years between the fifth and sixth.

These last two slim volumes could be mistaken for little postscripts. But closer study reveals *Mary Poppins in Cherry Tree Lane* as an exquisite cadenza,[1] and *Mary Poppins and the House Next Door,* as a true coda,[2] to all that has gone before.

So what has gone before? Close encounters, it seems, with those "worlds beyond worlds" of which the author speaks with such authority.

But there must be a way into these worlds, so where is the opening, the gateway, the "crack"? On the face of it, the characters in the stories are ordinary enough for the period—a middle-class family and their modest servant household. We have Mr. Banks, whose very name confirms that he goes to an office in the City every day and does something with money. There is Mrs. Banks, loving, flustered, ineffectual.

There are five children: Jane and Michael, twins John and Barbara, and baby Annabel; none of them is especially gifted or exceptionally awful. Then there are Mrs. Brill the comfortable cook, Ellen the sniffly housemaid, and Robertson Aye the gardener, who spends more time dozing in the broom cupboard, or using shoe polish to get a shine on Mr. Banks's bowler, than he ever does in mowing the lawn.

Nothing untoward. And yet it is to this conventional household that Mary Poppins comes. Could it be its very ordinariness which attracts her visitations?

A clue lies in the very first pages of the very first book. But it will take to the end of the third book, or even perhaps the fifth, to dawn on us that it is not the *children's* essential selves which half-remember another world, but their *father's* more than half-forgotten real self. This is the part of him, perhaps, which makes him so often crotchety, restless, and troubled.

It is always Mr. Banks who first notices the auguries: changes in the wind's direction, the first day of spring, the fact that his shaving water is always the right temperature when Mary Poppins is in residence.

It is Mr. Banks who spots the new star and, filled with unexpected tenderness, impulsively takes his wife in his arms and dances with her or lets his children lean on him on the window-seat as they stare up into the night sky. And it is Mr. Banks who, when Mrs. Banks complains that Mary Poppins has accepted the position of nanny "as if she were doing us a signal honor," replies, "Perhaps she is," and then swiftly withdraws again behind his newspaper.

He knows "in part," as St. Paul[3] put it, that there are "worlds beyond worlds, times beyond times"; but the everyday Mr. Banks doesn't know that he knows these things.

An excellent example of this is his shocking encounter at dusk with the white cat. We already know this cat has come to life from its china form on the nursery mantelpiece to roam the world seeking out those ("a king ... or a man going through the city streets") unafraid of returning the cat's gaze because that man—or king—"knows who he is."

"A white thing. Sort of leopard it was," gasps Mr. Banks all of a heap in the hall: "And *forget-me-nots* growing all over its fur . . . It—looked at me. A wild green look—right into my eyes. Then it nodded and said, 'Good evening, Banks!'"

He saw the magic creature, and, however briefly, sensed himself *seen*. This must at least mean he has the possibility of knowing who he really is, but the encounter has left his ordinary self in a state of terror and nervous collapse. Just as when some less visited part of him knew that the new star was Mary Poppins returning to her other world, Mr. Banks, as he trembles, "like a guilty thing surprised,"[4] doesn't know that he is "moving about in worlds not realized"[5]—just as his daughter, Jane, is beginning to do, and Michael, too, with his "obstinate questionings of sense and outward things."[6] Banks doesn't know that he is actually experiencing those "fallings from us,"[7] those "vanishings"[8] of which Wordsworth wrote so elegantly.

And yet, it will be Mr. Banks who, in the Park on Midsummer's Eve, will be suddenly "flooded with a sense of being . . . someone else who was, at the same time, himself." For a fleeting moment he is again a small boy, "standing tip-toe in button-up boots, his nose just reaching a glass-topped counter," to buy gingerbread from an ancient woman (that same Mrs. Corry, of course, from whom his children, unbeknownst to him, have not so long ago also bought gingerbread.) And behind him is "*someone wearing a straw hat with a flower or two springing from it.*"

And what about Mrs. Banks? As if to keep the center stage clear for Mary Poppins' entries and exits, the author gives the poor mother a very hard time. She is intimidated by her nanny, and for the most part is a loving, well-meaning, flustered woman who lives in the ordinary world seemingly unaware of the fabulous events forever taking place just behind her back. Only once for a brief but telling moment does a vestige of the Mary Poppins magic impinge on her consciousness— when she is stopped in her fussing tracks by the sound of a nightingale singing its heart out. (This nightingale has been transformed from its artificial existence on top of a music box by a cousin of Mary Poppins, a certain Mr. Twigley. Twigley's work seems to be to provide the world with all its music. That very afternoon he tuned Mrs. Banks' piano without so much as stepping outside his front door. "'A Nightingale!' sighs

Mrs. Banks dreamily. 'How very strange! They never sing in the city! I wish I knew where he came from!'"

That the author had an adoring and idealized memory of her own father, who died when she was seven, might go quite a long way to explain her sympathetic characterization of fathers in all her books. By the same token, perhaps it is because she was never a wife nor gave birth to a child that she portrays the mother in the *Mary Poppins* books (as well as in *Friend Monkey*) at second remove. One could probably argue equally that Mrs. Banks and Mary Poppins represent two aspects of the many faceted mother-archetype[9]: Mrs. Banks' relatively undeveloped character as the "Good Mother"[10] and Mary Poppins as the "Virgin Mother."[11]

Chronology, however, precludes any possibility that P.L. Travers was aware of Jungian work in this field until very late in her writing life. This fact not only goes to support Jung's conviction that there *is* such a thing as a "collective unconscious." It also, and more importantly, is a fine example of an artist drawing up the treasures of understanding from her own deep, mysterious well-spring, and perhaps rejoicing at a later date to learn that her findings are shared by others on the same deep search.

As for the children: of the five of them, the author focuses on the two eldest, Jane and Michael, who have attained the age of reason. Old enough at somewhere between seven and nine to engage with Mary Poppins, they are still young enough to teeter on the meandering thin line between the encroaching "shades of the prison house" and the light of "the vision splendid" of Wordsworth's *Ode*.[12] Jane ponders in her heart and wonders, and is in awe before the explained and the unexplainable. Michael is more brash, cheekier. Adoring Mary Poppins, he nevertheless badgers her with questions, takes risks with her, teases her, answers her back, and is always stepping over the line. The adventures and "education" of Jane and Michael make up a very large part of each book, so much so that at first sight one might consider the presence of John and Barbara and the baby, Annabel, as superfluous.

But not so, not so. They are there for a reason and are accorded chapters to themselves.

In the first book we find John and Barbara conversing merrily with the Starling as Mary Poppins tidies the nursery.

"I don't believe I'll ever understand Grown-ups," says John. ". . . For instance, they don't understand a word we say. But, worse than that, they don't understand what other things say. . . . Only last Monday I heard Jane remark that she wished she knew what language the Wind spoke . . ."

Mary Poppins tartly informs them that Jane—and Michael, too—did once understand the language of everything, but that as they grew older, they forgot.

"We won't forget," boast the Twins.
"You will," says Mary Poppins matter-of-factly.
"You will," sighs the Starling. "There never was a human being that remembered after the age of one . . . except *her* of course, but then she's the Great Exception . . . "

The Twins weep inconsolably, whereupon Mrs. Banks rushes in and comforts them. "There, there. Mother knows, Mother understands. . . . It will be all right when the teeth come through . . ."

In point of fact, Mother doesn't know; but as John says, "It was not her fault, poor woman, that she always said the wrong thing. It was just . . . that she didn't understand . . ."

Mother doesn't understand and so, of course, rejoices when the teeth do come through. But the Starling weeps when their talk turns to the babble of babes. He weeps for their loss of simplicity, of that one-fold-edness which is the true meaning of innocence.

"Who are you and where do you come from?" the Starling's fledgling child asks Annabel, "The New One" in *Mary Poppins Comes Back*. And between her "birth and her forgetting"[13] she answers the young bird in tones worthy of a sibyl:

"I am earth and air and fire and water. . . . I come from the Dark where all things have their beginning. . . . I come from the sea and its tides . . . from the sky and its stars . . . from the sun and its brightness . . . slowly I moved at first, always sleeping and dreaming. I remembered all I had been, and I thought of all I shall be. And when I had dreamed my dream I awoke and came swiftly. . . . I heard the stars singing as I came and I felt warm wings about me. I passed the beasts of the jungle and came through the dark, deep waters. It was a long journey . . ."

"A long journey, indeed!" said the Starling softly. "And, ah, so soon forgotten!"

"No!" says Annabel confidently. "I'll never forget . . . How could I ever forget?"

"Because they all do!" shrieks the Starling, "every silly human— except her," nodding his head at Mary Poppins. "She's the Oddity . . ."

And how Annabel weeps when the Starling is proved right. By the time her brothers and sisters are allowed into the nursery to admire her, she has forgotten; but unlike the child in the old Hindu tale who *knows* he has forgotten the place of his arising, this child has completely forgotten. And again the Starling sheds a tear for the loss of that true simplicity which is one-ness, wholeness.

So this is the ordinary enough family, each member in varying stages of sleep and awakening—which is perhaps why they are deemed worthy to be visited, from time to time, and taken in hand by Mary Poppins.

Mary Poppins.

She arrives first on the East Wind, then on a kite, and finally on a firework. She leaves first on the West Wind, then on a merry-go-round that spins off, turning into a star as it whirls up into the dark night sky, and lastly through an open door.

To look at, she is plain, not pretty, with "shiny black hair rather like a Dutch doll, thin, with large feet and hands and small, rather peering blue eyes, smelling always faintly of starch and toast."

Immaculate in her hat with the tulips, her parrot-headed umbrella tucked under one arm, feet turned out, nose turned up, "prim and trim," she is completely unsentimental, unbending, matter-of-fact, cool and collected at all times. There is absolutely nothing jolly, funny, or cozy about Mary Poppins. Not given to unnecessary chatter or kissing and cuddling, she does have occasional moments of tenderness; but above all, she is *always there*, strong, calm, reliable. She is always there to rescue the children when they have been suitably "punished" for bad moods and bad behavior by educative nightmares (the boys in the bowl who "kidnap" Jane; the awful cats who "kidnap" Michael) doubtless contrived by her in the first place. She is there as they fall with relief back on the pillows, there with warm milk and real reassurance that all is forgiven because all has been understood. The "punishment" has been harsh but fair and, at the last gasp, merciful.

Brusque as well as brisk, unbending, a "snappy dresser," extremely vain, with absolutely no sense of humor and easily offended, she never "tells anyone anything" and is a convincing incarnation of the author's deep understanding that not answering, not explaining leaves the possibility of going further. Throughout the books, Mary Poppins' answer to questions is almost always a glare, an icy stare, complete denial. In the teeth of considerable evidence—such as the imprint of the Sun's kiss on her cheek still there at breakfast-time after a night visit to a stellar circus, the gilt stars on the children's gingerbread ending up as real stars in the real sky, or Jane's handkerchief somehow finding its way round the knee of a boy in the china bowl on the mantelpiece—she always evinces total astonishment. She always is adamant in her denial that anything untoward, let alone magical, has happened. Only once, when she is caught out by Jane and Michael, does she permit herself, briefly, a warm, twinkling, conniving smile.

And yet generations of children have loved her. Some, in later years, even have spoken of her with heartfelt gratitude for having helped them through the vicissitudes of childhood.

What is she? The consistent still point at the center? A lodestar? A catalyst? Shamanistic because she acts as the conductor, the bridge between worlds? Virginal she certainly is, by the true definition of virgin as one who is whole, who has transcended the personal, and who is "pure in the sense that the attitude is uncontaminated by personal desirousness."[14] She is virginal because complete and therefore able to contain and sustain the many.[15]

What is evident is that when she is in residence at Number Seventeen Cherry Tree Lane she brings "worlds beyond worlds and times beyond times" with her.

A simple trip to the shops with Mary Poppins pushing the pram leads to buying gilt-starred gingerbread from Mrs. Corry (who, on her own admission, was well out of her teens when they were making this world, who knew Methusaleh in his cradle and was there when Columbus discovered America). Mrs. Corry seems to have held a particular fascination for the author, representing perhaps the crone of crones, an aspect of the female principle which interested her very much. Mrs. Corry isn't nice: She's positively scary, breaking off her barley sugar fingers and offering them to the twins. And she's perfectly horrid to her great galumphing daughters Annie and Fannie, who have to hold the ladders so that she and Mary Poppins can paste gilt stars onto the sky.

Buying balloons from another old crone leads to a positively Dionysian sky-ride along with all the friends, neighbors, and acquaintances who throng the books.

Tea is taken either on the ceiling with Uncle Albert or upside down with Mr. Turvey.

All this in broad daylight!

And at breakfast-time in the nursery, tell-tale signs of shoes wet with the dew, or the presence of starfish or stardust, betray the idea that everyone has been safely tucked up in bed all night.

These are just a few of the wonderful things which Jane and Michael know and know they have shared with Mary Poppins—things seen and heard and shared in in her company, things seriously magical and profoundly mysterious. But, when taxed by the children with these events—and taxed she is, across the books and in many chapters—she always denies that they happened. To say that she *denies* these magical or mysterious happenings is putting it mildly. Whenever questioned about them, she *explodes* with indignation—the righteous indignation of a plain, put-upon, ordinary, overworked nanny.

There is something thrilling, every time, for reader or listener, about this immense indignation which seems actually to lend its weight to the very truth of what we all know the children have experienced:

"I BEG your pardon!" she exclaims.

"All boundy and bouncy, rolling and bobbing on the ceiling? . . . Pasting stars to the sky? . . . Dancing on the sea floor? . . . In the Zoo at midnight? Animals *outside* the cages and humans *inside* the cages? ME! accepting a snakeskin belt from the Hamadryad? KITE? Am I to understand,

Michael Banks, that I came down from somewhere on the end of a piece of *string?* . . . Spinning round on top of music boxes? . . . Giving my jacket to a marble statue? . . . Nellie *Rubina?* One of Noah's daughters with the Ark in the Park? I helped her make the spring come? . . . Rescuing you from a planet full of fearful cats? . . . A red cow down the Lane in the middle of the city, looking for a lost star? . . . Christmas shopping with one of the Pleiades? . . . MY shadow with a butterfly on its shoulder and ME 'hopping about,' did you say, in the Park on Hallowe'en? Hallowe'en Party? HUMPH! The very idea! I have never been so insulted in my life! Never! . . . I'll have you know, I am a respectable person from a respectable family!"

This is the song, the refrain repeated over and over. We begin to wait for it with palpitating anticipation at the same time knowing, like Jane and Michael—and as the author herself allows in the great chapter, "Happy Ever After," in *Mary Poppins Opens the Door*—that as far as this so-called nanny is concerned "Appearances are Deceptive."

That very important chapter takes place on New Year's Eve—one of those magical pauses in our year (like Hallowe'en and Midsummer's Eve) of which the author makes full use. Mary Poppins has deigned to tell the children that the Old Year ends on the first stroke of twelve and the New Year begins on the last stroke of twelve.

Lying in his warm bed, Michael is watching Mary Poppins move about the nursery and "the crackling wing of her apron as she whisked about the room." When he has the nerve to ask her, "What happens in between the first stroke and the last stroke," the only answer he gets is: "Never trouble trouble till trouble troubles you." Quelled by the "Ominous Look" in her eye, Michael dives under the bedclothes. When he next pops up, what is Mary Poppins doing but taking all the soft toys the children usually go to bed with and propping them on the mantelpiece with a *book* in front of them. Phooey! Everybody knows toys can't read.

Of course Jane and Michael plan to stay awake to see the New Year in, and of course they fall asleep . . . only to awaken to the sound of all the bells of London Town—from St. Paul's steeple to the humblest chapel—ringing in the New Year. Then . . . silence . . . and then . . . "Boom!" said Big Ben. It was the first stroke of Midnight.

And the Crack opens, the Crack for which we all have nostalgia without always knowing it. The Crack where everything comes fully alive in the present moment, outside time. And, since this (we must never forget) is a story for *children,* the toys come to life, and all the well-loved characters from the Nursery Rhymes, Fairy Tales, and Favorite Books come tumbling off their pages: the Three Blind Mice dancing with the Farmer's Wife, Cock Robin with his Jenny Wren, the Cat and the Fiddle, Jack and the Giant ("they are bosom friends tonight"), the Sleeping Beauty, Cinderella, Robinson Crusoe and Man Friday, Goldilocks frolicking with the Three Bears, Kings and Queens and Humpty Dumpty, Goosey Goosey Gander, Giants and Fairies, Witches too, flying in on broomsticks, cackling their cacklingest. But "Nobody's frightened of them tonight." They're happy ever after because, as Sleeping Beauty tells the children:

> "Inside the Crack all things are as one. The eternal opposites meet and kiss. The wolf and the lamb lie down together,[16] the dove and the serpent share one nest. The stars bend down and touch the earth and the young and the old forgive each other. Night and day meet here, so do the poles. The East leans over towards the West and the circle is complete. This is the time and place, my darlings—the only time and the *only* place—where everybody lives happily ever after . . ."

Thus in *Mary Poppins Opens the Door,* which was originally intended to be the finale of a trilogy, the author presents what was at the very heart of all her seeking, yearning, questioning. It was at the heart of her best thought and her best feeling and would continue to be for the rest of her life: the fact and the mystery of this meeting and parting of opposites, the secret behind "Happy ever after." This pause, this conscious moment, here, now, is where all comes together in a flash, and is every time a "new beginning" before time once again takes command. Of course on the last stroke of twelve the Crack closes and we find ourselves tousled and troubled, rubbing our eyes against the morning sunlight of a new day in time to hear Michael ask the question for all of us:

"Shall we too, Mary Poppins?" (of course she had been there with them, at the *center* of the lawn, piping the tune, this time on a concertina).

"Shall you too, what?" she enquired with a sniff.

"Live happily ever afterwards?" he asked eagerly.

A smile, half sad, half tender, played faintly round her mouth.

"Perhaps," she said thoughtfully. "It all depends . . ."

What on, Mary Poppins?"

"On you," she said quietly, as she carried the crumpets to the fire.

And then there is the Park which figured nowhere in the film, but which has a book to itself. *Mary Poppins in the Park* is full of adventures which, we are exhorted by the author in her preface, "should be understood to have happened during any of the three visits of Mary Poppins to the Banks family." And she continues tartly, rather like her heroine: "This is a word of warning to anybody who may be expecting a fourth visit. She cannot forever arrive and depart . . ."

Surely the Park is macrocosm to Number Seventeen's microcosm? Or, dare one suggest, a microcosm to the cosmos itself?

Almost everyone from the Banks household appears in the Park at one time or another. Mary Poppins and the children, of course, are in and out of it nearly every day. Mr. Banks comes through it on his way home. The neighbors walk there: lonely Miss Lark with her dogs, blustery Admiral Boom with his long-suffering wife. Other lost souls are there too—the Mayor and his Aldermen, the Prime Minister, the absent-minded Professor—all always looking, looking for . . . Something.

And we must not forget the miserable Park Keeper, hidebound to the extreme by Bye-Laws and Regulations, bossing everyone about, fussing after dropped litter, times of opening, times of closing. Oh, how Mary Poppins derides and despises him! And oh, how he fights against the mystification and unease she brings about in him, stepping neatly as she does beyond the reach of any kind of Rules known to him.

The Park is the place where strange things happen while Mary Poppins sits "bolt upright against a tree," by the pram, innocuously darning socks or sewing on buttons: Neleus, the Marble Boy, steps off his plinth and plays with the children; Jane's miniature plasticine "park in the park" comes violently to life; the three lovely boys, Florimund, Veritain, and Amor (the unaffected, child-like incarnations of Beauty, Truth, and Love) step from the pages of a story-book. It is in the Park that Jane and Michael cross the threshold between "Here" and "There" and begin to wonder which of the two is more real, to understand that there is light and darkness and that for us there is no such thing or state or place as "Always." These are certainly some of the "great truths," which the author has said is what Mary Poppins has come to teach them. In almost every book, the Park is the scene of some sort of giddy gathering of swirling, whirling figures, dancing with their shadows, in some way liberated from their ordinary, everyday selves—which seems to be one of the author's favorite themes.

In *Mary Poppins in Cherry Tree Lane,* the penultimate book, the Park plays host to the Heavens themselves when they come down on Midsummer's Eve to dance the Grand Chain with mortal folk. This is the author's glorious cadenza, her "virtuoso passage," the moment where as much of the inner significance of these stories as will ever be revealed is revealed. Here we have nothing less than the meeting at *twilight* of counterparts, the coming together of halves, a *coniunctio oppositorum,* that absolutely fundamental, archetypal meeting of opposites studied and elucidated by such erudite luminaries as A.K. Coomaraswamy,[17] C.J. Jung,[18] and Mircea Eliade.[19]

The stars come down to earth, the higher comes down to the lower. The two meet and mingle at that special moment of our year. In this moment, in this story, all the lonely halves who were meant for one another without knowing it, find one another at last and join together with other happy couples. Everyone is with someone: the Prime Minister closeted with the King, the Keeper of the Zoological Gardens fishing for tiddlers in the pond with the Mayor and Aldermen, the Policeman and Ellen, the absent-minded Professor and Miss Lark happily paired, and Mr. Banks hurrying across the grass in answer to the call of his wife's sweet voice. Everyone is with someone—except the Park Keeper. Lonely past all bearing, he casts his Bye-laws to the winds, and himself upon the magic of the night and Old Wives' Tales. With arms outstretched and with cucumber behind his ears, he closes his eyes and, walking backwards, trusts he will "back into his own true love."

Surely his time has come? He must also be redeemable. After all, a book or two ago, he had had a flash of real understanding when he realized that "as far as his watchful eyes could see there were only two points of light in the dark night. 'That there star and the nightlight in Number Seventeen, if you look at 'em long enough you can hardly tell which is which . . .'" To which his mother, the Bird Woman, replies that one is the shadow of the other.

And now, on this most magical of Midsummer Eves, back and back he goes, step by step giving himself to the twilight, "Where was he? He dared not tell and dared not look. If he opened his eyes he might break the spell . . . Backward, backward, his destiny leading him." Backward, not forward . . . Unwinding himself from his habits, his ordinariness, his old ways? Who can say? "The Park Keeper felt lost and lonely. His outstretched arms were beginning to ache. His eyes were weary of seeing nothing. Even so, back and back he went . . ." Shedding the old onion skins of his narrow, frightened, restricted self, he stumbles on.

> . . . backward, backwards . . . was he even still in the Park? He heard behind him a distant murmur: nothing festive, no great clamor, merely friendly, sociable chatter of people at one with each other. . . Conversation went back and forth. How beautiful, the Park Keeper thought, was the sound of human gossip! Whoever these people were, he was sure, the longed-for "she" would be among them . . . And suddenly—bump! There she was! All he need do now was turn and face her. He swivelled round . . . and a firm hand thrust him sideways. 'I'll thank you not to behave like a carthorse. I am not a lamp-post!'[20] said Mary Poppins.

Mary Poppins! Park Keeper?! Oh no! Oh, dreadful moment of truth for both! That they could be each other's opposite? Denied and denied at every encounter, in every tart exchange. Now what will happen?

In the skilful hands of P.L. Travers—and with her perspicacious insight into universal Bye-laws and Regulations—Mary Poppins and the Park Keeper, unlike all the other halves of that evening, do not fall joyously re-united into one another's arms. No, they continue to produce in their irritation and scorn the necessary friction, the electrical charge of the overlap between the inner world and the outer world without which nothing will happen.

The Park Keeper, nonetheless, will never be the same. But his metamorphosis into himself is painful. Finding himself surrounded by the seeming chaos of the very Constellations leaping about in his Park, helping themselves to herbs and cherries, he cries out loud: "Everything's head over heels to-night. I don't know nothing no more!" And he goes away and hides himself from "the unbearable day and all its problems."

Only when the day has disappeared and "passed through its long blue *twilight* hour and had almost become night" does he awaken, just in time to see the Grand Chain coming to an end.

The Grand Chain: "Round and round. Right hand to right hand, left hand to left . . ." The stars dancing in a circle with "Mary Poppins, the two Banks children, Mrs. Corry, her daughters, the Bird Woman . . . Round and round. Hand to hand . . . Orion . . . Castor . . . Pollux . . . the Bear . . . the Fox."

He comes to himself and "like a man who has lost and regained his senses, he understood . . . He had forgotten what he had known . . . made it a thing of naught, something to be sneered at! He put his hands up to his eyes to hide the springing tears." As the dance comes to an end and the stars prepare to depart, he leaps up and joyfully offers them all the herbs they want, calling out wildly before he returns to himself: "Forgive me friends! I didn't reckernise you! I didn't reckernise myself . . . I forgot what I knew when I was a boy. It needed the dark to show things plain. But I know who you are now, all of you. And I know who I am. I am the Park Keeper with or without my hat."

At last! He is *himself* just as Mary Poppins is herself. "I am at home wherever I am," she boasts on the last page of the last book. All of a piece, light side, dark side. Herself. What we all wish to be.

And then she goes, through that "Other Door," that Open Door. Away she stalks through the nursery's reflection in the flames leaping high in the fireplace, through the Open Door glimmering on Miss Lark's next-door wall, and out into "the dark spreading night." The parrot-headed umbrella snaps open and up she soars, higher and higher: "a bright form glowing like a little core of light streaking through the darkness, cleaving a path, filling every watching heart down in the Lane with sudden sweetness.

"A shooting star!" cries Mr. Banks. "Wish on it children!". . .

"My dear Love!" Mr. Banks said tenderly as he touched Mrs. Banks's cheek. And they put their arms around each other and wished on the star.

Jane and Michael held their breath as the sweetness brimmed up within them. And the thing they wished was that all their lives they might remember Mary Poppins. Where and How and When and Why—had nothing to do with them. They knew that as far as she was concerned these questions had no answers . . . But in summer days to come and the long nights of winter, they would remember Mary Poppins and think of all she had told them. The rain and the sun would remind them of her, the birds and the beasts and the changing seasons. Mary Poppins herself had flown away, but the gifts she had brought would remain for always.

"We'll never forget you, Mary Poppins!" they breathed, looking up at the sky.

Her bright shape paused in its flight for a moment and gave an answering wave. Then darkness folded its wing about her and hid her from their eyes . . .

And then the author gently returns them to their father, who "pulls the curtains across the window and draws them all to the fire."

"It's gone," he says of the star with a great sigh; and "She's gone," the children must have whispered in themselves.

"She's gone," we echo. And close the book with a quiet smile, shared, we see, along with eyes bright with unshed tears, by our child or grandchild: sad but satisfied.

Gone, yet not gone, for she has left a far deeper imprint than the Mary Poppins of the film could ever make: She has left a door open, and, as she herself would say, it depends on us to keep it open. For Mary Poppins—who the author always insisted "just came" to her—knew, in the words of the German Romantic poet, Novalis, that only when

> *People who go about singing or kissing*
> *Know deeper things than the great scholars . . .*
> *When light and darkness mate*
> *Once more and make something entirely transparent,*
> *And people see in poems and fairy tales*
> *The true history of the world,*

only then will

> *our entire twisted nature . . . turn*
> *And run when a single secret word is spoken.*[21]

NOTES

1. "An outstanding virtuoso passage coming towards the end . . . of a movement." *Chambers Twentieth Century Dictionary.*
2. "The completion of a piece, rounding it off to a satisfactory conclusion." *Ibid.*
3. 1 Cor. 13: 9–12.
4. William Wordsworth, *Ode on Intimations of Immortality.*
5. *Ibid.*
6. *Ibid.*
7. *Ibid.*
8. *Ibid.*
9. See *Four Archetypes (Psychological Aspects of the Mother Archetype), extracted from The Archetypes and the Collective Unconscious,* Vol. IX, part 1 of *The Collected Works,* C.G. Jung, Routledge, Kegan Paul, 1972: "There are three essential aspects of the mother: her cherishing and nourishing goodness, her orgiastic emotionality, and her Stygian depths." Jung also defines the qualities associated with the mother archetype as "maternal solicitude and sympathy; the magic authority of the female; the wisdom and spiritual exaltation that transcend reason" but also "anything secret, hidden, dark, terrifying . . . inescapable."
10. See *The Great Mother: An Analysis of the Archetype,* Erich Neumann, Princeton University Press, Bollingen Series XLVII, 1955, where the "Good Mother's" attributes are considered to include the qualities of "containing, bearing, releasing, developing and nourishing," and the qualities of the "Virgin Mother" those of "transformation, inspiration, vision and ecstasy."
11. *Ibid.*
12. *Ode on Intimations of Immortality.*
13. *Ibid.*
14. Edward Edinger, *The Christian Archetype: A Jungian Commentary on the Life of Christ,* Inner City Books, Toronto, 1987. "There seems to be an archetypal

connection between virginity and the ability to handle transpersonal energy."
Also: "The virgin ego is one that is sufficiently conscious to relate to transpersonal energies without identifying with them."

15. "Only a virgin could contain a multitude." P.L. Travers in her annotations to Mircea Eliade's *The Two and the One,* Harper & Row: Torchbooks, New York, 1965.

16. Cf. Isaiah, 11:6 et seq.

17. ". . . for whatever is done *when it is neither day nor night* is done *ex tempore, sub specie aeternitas,* and *forever.*" Traditional Symbolism: Sundoor: Symplegades, from A. K. Coomaraswamy, *Selected Papers, Traditional Art and Symbolism,* ed. by Roger Lipsey, Bollingen Series LXXXIX, Princeton, 1977.

18. "The self as symbol of wholeness is a *coincidentia oppositorum* and therefore *contains light and darkness simultaneously.*" C.G. Jung, *Symbols of Transformation,* Vol. V, *The Collected Works,* Routledge & Kegan Paul, 1981.

19. ". . . the *coincidentia oppositorum* is to be seen in *orgiastic rituals aimed at the reversal of human behaviour and the confusion of values, in the mystical techniques for the union of contraries* . . . In general one can say that all these myths, rites . . . have the aim of *reminding men that the ultimate reality, the sacred, the divine defy all possibilities of rational comprehension . . . that the divine ground (Grund) can only be grasped as a mystery, a paradox . . . an absolute freedom beyond Good and Evil.*" Mircea Eliade, *The Two and the One,* Harper & Row, 1965.

20. *Mary Poppins in Cherry Tree Lane,* p. 24 et. seq.

21. "When Geometric Diagrams . . .", Novalis, 1800 (trans. by Robert Bly in *News of the Universe: Poems of twofold consciousness,* chosen and introduced by Robert Bly, Sierra Club Books, San Francisco, 1980).

HOW ARE THEY GOING TO MAKE THAT INTO A MUSICAL?

P. L. Travers, Julie Andrews, and Mary Poppins

by Brian Sibley

WALT DISNEY'S film *Mary Poppins* found an immediate place in the hearts of cinema-goers that has never been dislodged. It is—along with *The Wizard of Oz* and Disney's other classic *Snow White and the Seven Dwarfs*—one of the most beloved family films ever made.

Mary Poppins won all kinds of awards, including six Oscars, and is generally acknowledged as being not just Disney's last critical and financial triumph but, indeed, one of his all-time greatest pictures. It is, quite simply, one of those films about which people have incredibly warm and affectionate feelings.

P.L. Travers, on the other hand, had rather different feelings about the film which she expressed quite openly to me on many occasions. It has to be said, however, that our first communication on the matter was brief. In a letter dated 10 December 1968 (at which time I was researching a biography of Disney) Pamela Travers wrote:

> I am afraid there is very little I can say to you about Walt Disney. I did not care very much for the film he made of my books. Generally because, although it was a colorful entertainment, it was not true to their meaning. Nor do I like what he does with the Fairy Tales, so I don't think I am a very useful person for your study. However, I can say I think the Mickey Mouse and other cartoons are splendid entertainment for the general public and I used to enjoy these myself very much . . .

A few years later, undaunted, I wrote to her again about the film when it looked as if the Disney biography might eventually be published (unfortunately it *wasn't!*). Pamela's letter is undated, but subsequent correspondence dates it as being in the late summer of 1972. On this occasion, she was more forthcoming:

> I remained quiet about the Poppins film for a number of reasons. One, it seemed unkind to speak out after Walt Disney had died, for his death was a brave one and somehow I could not do it. Also, I don't want to offend them for we are inextricably linked, alas, by the contract . . .

I had asked her about an alleged "Conversation with the Author" which appeared in the souvenir brochure for the film and which implied that the finished film had P.L. Travers' unhesitating approval. Her response was suitably fiery:

> I yesterday wrote and demanded that the "Conversation with the Author" which appears in the brochure of the film be deleted for the next round of the film (in June 1973), even if they have to burn a million copies. So many people have written to me and asked me if it was true. Of course it is a pack of lies . . .

Spurred on, perhaps, by her annoyance with Disney, Pamela composed a statement that I could quote in my book ("But please do not use it until you show me in what context it will be placed. This is important. So do please abide by this."). Her letter continued with comments that, while not part of the prepared statement, are themselves very revealing. First she commented on a remark I had made in my letter to the effect that the huge worldwide success of the film must have increased international sales of the Poppins books:

> Yes, I think my publishers would say that the film had helped the sale of the books, though it has to be remembered that the books were best sellers in most languages before the film came out. It had an audience prepared for it. And many people who truly love the books tell me that they felt the film had not entirely lost the spirit of them. But how much better a film it would have been had it carefully stayed with the true version of Mary Poppins! Her very plainness would have given it drama, for she herself would shine through . . .

Pamela then spoke of some of the things she most disliked about the film:

> All had to be sweetness and light and *cruelty* in order to get the senti-mental outcome at the end. I pleaded with the Disneys not to let Mr. Banks tear up the poem. No good. And they never told me Mrs. Banks was to be a suffragette. I had suggested to Disney that it be set in Edwardian times—in that way it could never be out of date—but I never guessed he would gild the lily with Women's Suffrage . . .

The statement which she enclosed with this letter touched on these and other aspects of the way in which her books had been transferred to the screen. As it is perhaps the clearest indication of her views on the film, it bears reprinting in full:

> The first thing one has to do, I think, in pondering upon the relation of the film to the book, is to ask oneself what the book is about. Its chief character is a young woman who arrives, apparently from nowhere, and proceeds to impose upon a small, modest, chaotic household her own ideas of order. Having achieved this and, in the process, introduced the children to a world of magic, she takes off, again apparently for nowhere, by means of a parrot-headed umbrella. It is as simple as that.
>
> As to the film—I am well aware that books have to undergo some sort of sea-change when they are translated to the screen. Magic, conveyed in a book by words and the silence between words, inevitably, in a film, becomes trick. The ear is subtler than the eye. Even so the questions remain.
>
> How, for instance, did it happen that the little house in Cherry Tree Lane transformed itself into a mansion, with the household undergoing the same enlargement? What wand was waved to turn Mr. Banks from a bank clerk into a minor president, from an anxious, ever-loving father into a man who could cheerfully tear into pieces a poem that his children had written? How could dear, demented Mrs. Banks, fussy, feminine and lov-ing, become a suffragette?
>
> Why was Mary Poppins, already beloved for what ·she was—plain, vain and incorruptible—transmogrified into a soubrette? For what reason was Bert, a subsidiary figure in the book, elevated into the position of the fam-ily's reconciling factor, instead of Mary Poppins? And how was it that Mary Poppins herself, the image of propriety, came to dance a can-can on the roof-top displaying all her underwear? A child wrote, after seeing the film, "I think Mary Poppins behaved in a very indecorous manner." Indecorous,

indeed! Of course, a can-can would be well within Mary Poppins' provenance, if she felt like dancing it but nothing is more certain—if she did—than that her skirts would, of their own accord, cling modestly round her ankles.

The ways of film-makers are strange. It is as though they took a sausage, threw away the contents but kept the skin, and filled that skin with their own ideas, very far from the original substance. They try to "improve" upon what is, no matter how much or for how long that "What is" has already been tried and tested. And, it must be admitted, that along their own lines, they often succeed. The film of *Mary Poppins,* with all its glamour and splendors and the devoted energy of its cast, has been a tremendous success. But if we are comparing book and film, the sea-change is also tremendous.

Fifteen years later, finding myself working with fellow film historian, Richard Holliss, on *another* book about Disney (which, this time, *was* published!), I wrote again to Pamela for permission to quote from that statement. "My first feeling," she wrote back on 7 February 1987, "on reading your letter and re-reading my own comments on the *Mary Poppins* film was 'Let the sleeping—even the dead—dog lie.' Values since our correspondence, have become even more devalued . . ." Nevertheless, I was invited to visit her to in order to talk things over. As a result, a much-edited extract from her statement appeared in *The Disney Studio Story,* published in 1988.

Having met, however, we became firm friends. Before long, we found ourselves working together on a film project for Disney with the provisional title *Mary Poppins Comes Back*—although sadly, in the end, she never *did!*

A few facts about the process by which the original *Mary Poppins* found its way onto the screen may be informative. Walt Disney had first become aware of the stories when they were read by his daughters, Diane and Sharon. It was the late 1940s and, immediately sensing their movie potential, he began trying to acquire the film rights.

At first—indeed for a considerable period of time—Pamela Travers resisted the idea: "His offers," she told me in a letter dated 21 September 1972, "were along the lines of a cartoon & that I couldn't accept. It was only when he came up with the idea of a live cast that I began to be interested." Walt's brother and business partner, Roy Disney, visited the author in New York and explained how the film might be made using a combination of animation and live-action similar to the technique employed in *Song of the South,* the studio's successful 1946 film version of the "Uncle Remus" stories. But it was only when Walt himself called to see Pamela, during one of his visits to London in the 1950s, that the project began look as if it might happen.

Author and film-maker got on well with one another, and Pamela Travers was much struck by Disney's charisma. "It was," she once told me, "as if he were dangling a watch, hypnotically, before the eyes of a child." Nevertheless, it was to be a further ten years before she finally relinquished the film rights, and then only on condition that she should have a role as the film's consultant. It is an indication of Walt's passion to film *Mary Poppins* that he pursued the rights for so long and agreed to a hitherto unprecedented arrangement of allowing the original author a voice in the making of the film.

It was decision he was later to regret, for there were many tempestuous meetings between Pamela Travers, Walt Disney, and the team responsible for turning the stories into a musical film: writers Don Da Gradi and Bill Walsh along with song-smiths Richard M. Sherman and Robert B. Sherman. The Sherman brothers turned out a song score containing numbers that were to become known all over the world, but which singularly failed to satisfy the author, who could not understand why they didn't use existing music such as "Greensleeves" and "Tarara-boom-de-ay"!

During many weeks of meetings—all of which were recorded on tape—the author made endless suggestions, comments, and criticisms in the most acerbic of Traverish language. She addressed the interpretation of Mary Poppins' character, the middle-class English-ness of the settings, and the vocabulary that the different characters should and should not use. ("'Hiring and firing' are Americanisms. We would use 'engaged and dismissed.'") A few of her suggestions were adopted, but the majority were not. And the film was made without her further involvement.

Even though Pamela Travers had a good many reservations about the completed film, she had nothing but personal praise for the actress who played the eponymous heroine. In one letter written in 1972, she spoke of Julie Andrews as having "integrity and a true sense of comedy" and added: "I think [she] would willingly have put on a black wig and turned up her nose had the director required it. . . . But he didn't require it . . ." In another letter, dated 5 September 1972, she wrote:

> I have such a high opinion of Julie Andrews as a true professional & believe that, if asked by the director to look like the Mary Poppins of the books she would have come as near to it as she humanly could. But, alas, she was not asked to be much more than sweet & pretty. Even so, there were moments in the film that showed that she understood, even though not allowed to express, the essential quality of the original . . .

In a conversation with me in the spring of 1998, Julie Andrews recalled her work on the film. She began with her memories of the author, whom she first encountered on the other end of a telephone line: "I had only just given birth to my daughter Emma about thirty-six hours before. Suddenly the phone rang, and they said there was a Mrs. P.L. Travers on the line for me. I thought: 'I'd better speak to her, but doesn't anyone know that I have just given birth and am feeling a bit weary?'" When the phone call was put through, Julie Andrews experienced a typically brisk Travers conversation:

> "Hello, this is P. L. Travers. Is this Julie Andrews?"
> "Yes . . ."
> "Well, talk to me! I want to hear what you sound like!"
> "Well, what can I tell you, Mrs. Travers? I'm very thrilled, I believe I'm going to be doing the film . . ."
> "Well, you've got the nose for it, that's for sure. You're too pretty, but you've got the nose for it!"

Later, actress and author met: "I went to tea—a very formal tea at her house in London. I liked her. She was an eccentric and rather tough old bird, but a good-hearted one, I felt. But she was very worried about what they were going to do and having subsequently written children's books myself, I would also be worried."

The story of Julie Andrews' involvement in the film began in the late fall of 1961, when Walt Disney went to see her in the Broadway production of *Camelot*. She was not, in fact, his first choice for the role of Mary Poppins. He had wanted Mary Martin, who had starred in the Broadway versions of *South Pacific* and *The Sound of Music;* but while being a legendary stage performer, Martin had no wish to make films and Disney had to look elsewhere. It was Walt's secretary who, having seen *Camelot,* suggested to her boss that he should consider Julie Andrews and go to see the production when he was next in New York.

This he did and, after the show, went backstage. Having expressed his admiration for her performance as Queen Guinevere—but with no further preamble—Walt Disney on the spot asked Julie to appear in his forthcoming movie, *Mary Poppins.* At that time, however, it was impossible for her to commit to the project. *Camelot* still had three months to run, following which Julie was to have a baby.

Walt assured Julie that the film could wait, but invited her to visit his studio in Burbank, California, and look at some of the preparatory work which had been done on the picture. So, as soon as she could following the closure of *Camelot,* Julie Andrews and her then husband, designer Tony Walton, flew to Hollywood.

For the young actress, it was an exciting but anxious time. To be offered a film debut starring in the title role of a major movie was enticing, but daunting: "Much as I had always wanted to go into films, I thought: 'Gosh! Can I make a movie? Will I be able to do it justice? Will I be any good at it?'"

In addition, Julie had never read any of the books on which the film was to be based: "I very quickly acquainted myself with them. At that time, if I had any reservations it would have been that the books were so perfectly written in their primness, so boxed-in with rigid disciplines, that I thought, 'Now, how are they going to make *that* into a musical?' But, of course, the way they did it was simply miraculous."

Once at the Disney Studio, Julie was instantly captivated by the ideas being developed for the film. She was particularly fascinated by the "storyboards": thousands of sketches telling the story of the film in pictorial form—similar to a comic strip—that were pinned-up on large boards around the studio. "You get a real idea of the flow of the film," she recalls, "and it was so exciting, because I had an immediate impression as to how the film was going to look."

There were also a number of remarkable song-and-dance numbers that were instantly attractive to the singer: "The thing that was wonderfully appealing was the music and dance. I didn't know the work of Bob and Dick Sherman until that first day at the Disney Studio, but it was so fresh and charming that I thought, this is just fine! I couldn't find anything wrong with it."

In fact, the Sherman brothers' songs (of which there were then more than thirty, later distilled to the seventeen numbers in the finished film) struck an immediate chord with Julie Andrews: "My background, long before I had been on Broadway, was vaudeville and music-hall, and the songs they played to me had a wonderfully 'rum-tee-tum' vaudeville quality about them. 'Jolly Holiday' and 'Supercalifragilistic [expialidocious]' were good old, knock-down, drag-out music-hall songs! I loved them, and thought I could not only do justice to them but I would have such fun! Mind you, 'Supercalifragilistic[expialidocious]' was so fast that it was almost impossible to sing and dance at the same time!"

There were also the beautiful ballads: "Chim Chim Cher-ee," "Feed the Birds," and the lullaby, "Stay Awake" with its truly Poppinsish reverse-logic: Tell children who won't go to sleep to stay awake and *then* they'll go to sleep!

The final incentive for Julie Andrews to accept the role of Mary Poppins was Walt's invitation to Tony Walton to design the costumes for the movie: "It was a wonderful offer for Tony and launched his career in films. In fact, Walt was so pleased with his costume designs, that he had him design the set for Cherry Tree Lane and the interiors of the Banks household. There we both were, working together on our very first movie!"

It is a testament to Walt Disney's skills as a showman that he sought out talent and gave it his backing. *Mary Poppins* was the Sherman brothers' first full-scale musical, it had with a first-time designer, and it was featuring an actress who was making her first appearance in a film.

Whereas Jack Warner had been too fearful of casting Julie Andrews to play Eliza Doolittle in *My Fair Lady* (the role she had successfully created on the New York and London stage) and opted instead for the established (but non-singing) Audrey Hepburn, Walt Disney chose a performer with no experience in front of the camera, trusted her with the key role in his most ambitious picture, and made her into an Oscar-winning film star.

To begin with, it was all rather nerve-wracking: "The very first scene that I ever made on film was one leading into the 'Jolly Holiday' sequence. Bert said: 'Mary Poppins, you look bea-utiful!' and I had to say, 'Do you really think so?' All I could think was: 'How do I say that? What am I going to do? Will it look all right?'"

Once filming had begun, Julie Andrews kept in touch with P.L. Travers, updating the author (who despite her billing as "Consultant" had long ceased to be consulted) on how things were progressing. One such undated letter follows, published here with Miss Andrews' kind permission. Brimming over with behind-the-scenes news and gossip, her letter conveys the actress' huge enthusiasm and excitement with the project.

Julie Andrews writes warmly of her co-star Dick Van Dyke, of the veteran vaudevillian Ed Wynn, and of Karen Dotrice and Matthew Garber—the two youngsters playing the Banks children. The letter is mostly self-explanatory to anyone who has seen the film, but a couple of references need a little clarification.

Admiral Boom (played in the film by Reginald Owen) was originally to have been served by *two* boatswains (the "Mr. Binnacle" of the books, plus a "Mr. Barnacle"). The Admiral was also to have sung a song which had the chorus: "Time has been my watchword / Punc-tu-al-i-ty / Tho' the world takes its time from Greenwich / Greenwich takes *its* time from me!"

A number of sequences were planned only to be later abandoned. One such sequence was inspired by the "Bad Tuesday" chapter in P.L. Travers' *Mary Poppins* in which the children accompany Mary Poppins on a trip around the world using a magic compass. Various songs were written for this sequence including "The North-Pole Polka," "The Land of Sand" (which with different lyrics found its way into *The Jungle Book* as Kaa's hypnotic song, "Trust in Me"), and "Beautiful Briny" (which finally ended up in *Bedknobs and Broomsticks*). As for "The Chimpanzoo"—the excision of which clearly delighted both actress and author!—this was to have been based on the "Full Moon" chapter, in which the children accompany Mary Poppins on a night-time visit to the zoo, where they see animals walking about looking at human beings in cages. The song began: "In Timbuctoo / There's a Chimpanzoo / That's run by Chimpanzees / It's an oddish place / Where the human race / Is under lock and key."

And Julie Andrews' comment about "my lullaby" being "back *in!*" refers to Mary Poppins' song "Stay Awake," which was at one point to have been cut from the film. Pamela Travers wrote and protested the planned cut. Shortly afterwards, the song was reinstated.

Letter from Julie Andrews to Pamela Travers:

10459 Sarah St.
North Hollywood
Wednesday

Dear Mrs. Travers—

I've been meaning to write to you for *so* long. In fact, I *did* start a letter to you—but by the time I got around to finishing it, it was so out of date. I decided to scrap it—and start again.

We're really working like fiends at the moment—& it's all very exciting & new—but *oh* so slow! If we manage to get forty seconds worth of film at the end of a day we are doing pretty well—& it's hard to practice my singing. I'm so anxious to get into the "meatier" bits. We have done a great deal of the Jolly Holiday sequence (you know—the animated bit)—& almost all of the tea party at Uncle Albert's. I think that will look simply marvelous—& very funny.

Ed Wynn is delightful as Uncle Albert—very dear—and *so* happy. And Dick Van Dyke is grand as Bert. He's extremely winning—&

I like to think that he & I look well together on the screen.

Gosh—there are so many things to tell you—I hardly know what to write about next!!

The children look adorable—Michael has the most expressive face—& somehow everything he says seems amusing. Jane is sweet—& quite a good little actress. We have slight problems with Michael—for he *hates* heights—& all the flying stuff in Uncle Albert's has been very trying for him—& we've had tears once or twice. But everyone is most kind—& the children are treated terribly well—& with a great deal of respect. No "talking down"!

You knew, didn't you, that Admiral Boom's song had been cut? It's a great relief—for we felt that it held up the film. And he only has one Barnacle (or Binnacle) now—not both. So that's good.

The chimpanzoo is out—hooray, hooray!!—& best of all—my lullaby is back *in!* Your letter did the trick I think—though don't say I said so!

I recorded it yesterday. The orchestrations are really lovely—& all of the songs are working into the scenes very well now.

Tony's costumes are a delight—& I'm so proud to wear them. And his sets are beginning to look *very* pretty—especially Cherry Tree Lane.

As for me . . . —well! I hardly know *what* I'm at! Filming is so very different from anything I've ever done. Nothing (so far) has been shot in sequence—not even the shots within a scene. So it's very hard to try & imagine what it will look like when it's all pieced together. But I'm enjoying it all immensely—though most of our filming has been the "trick" photography—flying, floating, jumping etc. We're supposedly ahead of schedule just a little—& everyone seems very happy about it all. . .

We're really very happily settled in over here. Our house is roomy and comfortable—Emma is simply *adorable* & looks brown and bonny. And it's lovely to have Tony back here again.

Please excuse my atrocious scribble—this letter is written in the half dark on the set—& I have to keep popping up to rehearse etc.

Tony & I send all our love to you—& hope that you're well & happy.

Please don't worry about anything—I really do think that on the whole you'd be pleased with the way things are going . . .

Love,

as always

from

Julie

In her long letter to me about *Mary Poppins* back in 1972, Pamela Travers wrote: "I hope some day to tell the whole story." This hasn't been quite the *whole* story, but it certainly represents a good few chapters of it . . .

PART THREE

THE OTHER BOOKS

HANUMAN IN PUTNEY

by James George

DURING THE half-century of her writing career, P.L. Travers dipped her pen in the wisdom-well of traditional stories and myths. She did so judiciously, eschewing the obvious "interpretations" of the gleanings of another culture. Instead she set herself the more demanding task of finding the essential inner threads of meaning within an ordinary Western setting. How else to make the ordinary extraordinary, not merely exotic? The extraordinary can be made real in a way that the exotic never can. For only the real can truly move us.

Travers shows us that myths are to be read as stories about reality, in which moments of connection to the source of life redeem and transform. These stories are journeys for the reader, which start by our seeing clearly and accepting totally where we actually are at this moment, for this is our present reality. Starting anywhere else than here and now is off the mark.

She also shows us that, like all true teachers, myths and fairy tales invite us to search deeper for hidden meanings, for an understanding that goes beyond words. To try to convey these meanings in a modern setting is a daunting undertaking, and very few have succeeded. Magical tales did not begin with the Jataka stories and the Thousand and One Nights; nor did they end with the brothers Grimm. The Mary Poppins books, I would contend, have that elusive quality and have been recognized by three generations of readers. The other major work of P.L.

Travers, *Friend Monkey,* is still awaiting recognition but should, I believe, be considered. For it demonstrates, as do the Mary Poppins books, how myths can be brought to life where we actually live it—for Travers, in London.

Friend Monkey moves from the extraordinary to the ordinary and back again. It begins and ends on a magical "no-place" tropical island that is not on any map and that not everyone can see. Most of the action is in London's Putney district, a neighborhood which seems at first sight to be hardly a promising locale for a story that could have been given all the sentimental, romantic—and, for most of us, unreal— embellishments of a setting in the Himalayas or Ceylon. Compared to the modest affluence of Mary Poppins' Banks family, the Linnet family lives in a state of financial stringency and could never dream of hiring a nanny. Instead, a monkey appears mysteriously, to serve them—and to test them.

In traditional cultures, the mythical tale has many levels to challenge our comprehension of its meaning. There is the outer or obvious exter- nal meaning and there are—waiting for those who have ears to hear and eyes to see—secret, inner, or hidden meanings.

The outer level of *Friend Monkey* begins in 1897, Queen Victoria's Jubilee year. We find a shipping clerk in the Port of London surprising himself by impulsively deciding, against all reason, to adopt a young monkey that has been smuggled aboard a cargo ship and is about to fall into the clutches of a villain who would sell the poor monkey to some zoo or circus. On being admitted to the Linnet household, the monkey cannot do enough for the family to repay them for their kind- ness. Indeed his zeal to help both infuriates everyone and at the same time endears him to them. No one can deny his good intentions, how- ever catastrophic the practical consequences.

As the tale unfolds, life in London becomes more and more unbear- able for the Linnets, thanks to the benevolent activities of their new friend Monkey. Soon, with the loss of his job and no prospect of find- ing another, Mr. Linnet decides to emigrate with his family to Equatorial Africa where a friend has connections. But their ship sinks and they find themselves castaways on a mysterious tropical island, where all their basic needs are provided by an abundant nature and where, it seems, animals from zoos and circuses are being returned to the wild by an international conspiracy of "animal fanciers." This conspiracy is headed by the Scottish Professor McWhirter, whom we had all mistaken for a villain at the beginning of the story.

To understand other layers of meaning, it would help to have some acquaintance with the story of Hanuman as told in the great Indian epic, the *Ramayana*. We might read *Friend Monkey* without recognizing its mythological origins if Travers had not already told us, on the cover, of the connection to this epic tale. Thus forewarned, the reader is able to recognize, towards the end of the book, that Professor McWhirter's story of a monkey king comes straight out of the *Ramayana*:

> It's a story of a hero-god, wounded in battle, needing herbs. And a monkey lord leaping away and bringing back part of the Himalayas. A sprig o' green was all was needed, but—unable to do a thing by halves—he had to bring back a whole mountain! . . . And for that the hero rewarded him: a jewel to hang in the midst of his forehead and others to hang around his neck. And since that time—once in many a year—there's a monkey born with white on his brow and a patch of white around his throat to show where the jewels were. And the monkeys take him for their king— or so the auld wives tell us.

Other levels of understanding are, of course, more deeply hidden, and we are given only a few discrete clues to aid our own search. The last chapters set on the tropical island "that is not on any map" are richly laced with inner meanings. For example, there is the theme of "losing and finding": Mr. Linnet happily throws away his bowler hat and London boots, only to have them promptly returned to him by his ever faithful friend, Monkey. Linnet sighs, but accepts—not just the boots and the bowler, but himself.

It is also near the end of the book that "the One and Only" Professor McWhirter explains to Mr. Linnet *Friend Monkey*'s need to repay him for all his kindness. McWhirter points to the need for acceptance—of oneself and of the other—and to the duty not only of learning to love, but of letting oneself *be* loved. Yet these hints are so understated they are easily missed.

In an undated letter to my wife Carol and myself, which she sent us along with a copy of *Friend Monkey* in December, 1972, Travers reveals something of her hidden intent.

> You know how long I have brooded on Hanuman. The book is about that aspect of him (not him but as it were a thousandth descendant of his) that is excessive, that can't do anything by halves, the ever-loving and self-forgetting creature that because of his ever-love creates difficulties inevitably in the world around him; and his effect on the human beings who minister to him. Maybe it's a book about learning to love. Very simple and because of its slight flavor of mythology the Americans can't understand it, I think, though its going well in England where they are more natively familiar with such things. Anyway, remembering Hanuman, you may perhaps find something in it.

Later she wrote to us: "I have lived with one monkey (and he a lord) for so long that the monkey ways have become part of me. If we all have our own myth, as it is said, then mine is Hanuman."

Travers had already written about this some twenty years earlier in "The Fairy Tale As Teacher." There she describes an ancient store of knowledge which can be pictured as a central source of light, or fire, which sends occasional shafts down on our troubled world. She cites the *Vedas,* the *Mahabharata,* and the *Ramayana* as manifestations of this knowledge. She goes on to suggest that, in all the world's store of fairy tales, we will never find the like of Hanuman, the Monkey King, who was so simple, so noble, so ready to serve Rama. Nowhere else, she states, does the "instructive fire" bring together such opposites as the impetuous ape and he who maintains the very cosmos.

Unlike the four Mary Poppins books, which seem almost to have written themselves, the three books of the *Friend Monkey* cycle were both much longer in gestation and harder work for their author, as she had lost the original manuscript and had had to rewrite the entire book while writer-in-residence at Claremont University in California. On the eve of her first visit to us in Ceylon in October, 1963, Travers had written to us of her desire to come to what is now called Sri Lanka "to smell and sense the world of Hanuman whose story I love and about whom I am writing." Carol helped her find a beautiful centuries-old bronze statue of the monkey god in the antique market of Colombo. Pamela joyfully took this bronze Hanuman back to London with her, and it was still in a place of honor at her home in Chelsea when I last visited her in 1994.

Friend Monkey was not published until 1971, at least eight years after its conception. Together with *Friend Monkey's Friend* and *Friend Monkey's Kingdom,* the story runs to more than three hundred pages— the only long story Travers published after the *Mary Poppins* books. For the public, it never quite recaptured the magic of *Mary Poppins,* but that is a high standard by which to measure any book. Perhaps she worked at it too hard, thinking it through, whereas Mary Poppins came to her more intuitively and naturally. Or perhaps she was right when she complained that the minds of the young are "so unfurnished" that they lack the associations which could resonate with the great myths of world culture. Reading *Friend Monkey* without knowing the story of Hanuman is like trying to play the Indian sitar with half its resonating strings missing.

In any case, there can be no doubt that Travers was disappointed by the tepid reception of *Friend Monkey,* especially in the United States. She wrote to us early in 1973 from New York:

> Here it is not understood except by rare people. . . . I feel that I have written a sort of testament. In England it is much better understood but the U.S. reception has thrown me into the deeps. That something so clear, so obviously to do with love and loving isn't seen! So that I have lost a lot of faith in myself. Am I a writer? Do I know anything about the myths? Who am I? And what? Shall I ever write anything else? (This is a common sickness among writers but I am having a bad bout of it and no medicine or reassurance seems to assuage it. I need a whole new set of impressions, I expect.)

Of course, she did recover, and went on to write two more books in the *Mary Poppins* series and more than fifty essays which appeared in *Parabola* and other magazines during the next two decades.

At the deepest level, all truly creative work draws its inspiration from a higher level than that of ordinary life, a consciousness than is quite distinct from our automatic associations that go on all the time in each of us. Perhaps the function of myth and art in a traditional culture is to remind and reconnect us to that consciousness which is dormant in us, waiting to be awakened and transformed by the touch of love. So many myths turn around this theme. The tragedy of our contemporary Wasteland is that we are no longer connected with that which could awaken us; we have become Flatlanders, lacking any contact with what can vivify our search for meaning and for life.

In the three decades since *Friend Monkey* was first published, however, we have come some distance towards reconnecting our culture with its mythological roots. Our minds are less unfurnished than they were. Perhaps we are ready to take a fresh look at *Friend Monkey* today and see more than we did when we first read it.

If it does seem more meaningful now, we have to thank, among others, Mircea Eliade, Ananda Coomaraswamy, Joseph Campbell, and (not least) Pamela Travers for having helped us to bridge the gap that had been killing us for so long—the perilous gap between the ordinary and the extraordinary, the profane and the sacred, the ego and the "I am." For only when I am reconnected, if only for a moment, with what I really am can I begin to learn to love.

It was not for nothing that on October 31, 1966, when Travers was asked to speak at the Library of Congress in Washington, D.C., she took as her theme the epigraph of E.M. Forster's *Howard's End,* "Only Connect . . ."

> It's the theme of all Forster's writing, the attempt to link a passionate skepticism with the desire for meaning; to find the human key to the inhuman world about us; to connect the individual with the community, the known with the unknown; to relate the past to the present and both to the future. . . . Thinking is linking.

As the numbers increase of those who are ready to hear the mature wisdom Travers has distilled for us, as the bee makes honey, I expect that *Friend Monkey* will now be more widely appreciated.

"Thinking is linking," Travers tells us. But what are we to think of Friend Monkey's overdoing? Can there not be too much thinking—and not enough linking?

The intrepid anthropologist, Miss Brown-Potter answers: "It is better to do too much than too little. Much can always be whittled down. But little can be done with little."

And so we leave the Linnet family, and the monkey king who wants only to serve, in their rediscovered tropical garden of Eden, with the word, thrice repeated, which concludes the book:

HALLELUJAH!

From Teheran, I wrote to Travers, asking her about the meaning of this word, Hallelujah. On February 28, 1973, she replied:

> It is a Hebrew word for a song of praise but to me it is much more than that. If you say the vowels quickly, giving them the French pronunciation, AEIOU, you will get Hallelujah. . . . You remember that Beelzebub [in Gurdjieff's *Beelzebub's Tales to his Grandson*] speaks of the Sacred Aeioua, Remorse. . . . Well, to praise, perhaps one should have first had remorse and it seems to me that the vowels are the fundamental sound of the cosmos, the consonants are related to individual planets. This is only my idea, mind you.

And even here—"mind you"—Travers, never one to attach too much meaning to a single explication, leaves the door open for a new thought.

At the end of her preface to the 1987 edition of *Friend Monkey* Travers asks: "But what are words? One can say more—or as much— by a look or a gesture. Silence is one of the subtlest forms of communication. It is full of secrets and possibilities." And one of those possibilities is to write a book about a hero who never says a word but has so much to communicate!

ABOUT THE SLEEPING BEAUTY

The Veil Grows Transparent—Or Does It?

by Martha Heyneman

" L ET IT drop into you like a stone."

That was the advice Pamela Travers gave to a small group of us she was helping with the study of fairy tales. We clamored for analyses, explanations—What does this story *mean?*

But she merely advised us to keep a book of fairy tales on the bedside table, read one every night before falling asleep, and "Let it drop into you like a stone."

She even told us a cautionary tale—doubly illuminating, because we experienced how much deeper the answer to a question goes when dramatized in the language of story than when spelled out in the abstract language of the univalent intellect. The story echoes around in the body, and—regardless of our chronological age—in the intense emotions of our childish essence. This essence wants desperately not to be the object of ridicule like the man in the story, and so is emotionally motivated to follow the course the tale-teller has been recommending—but recommending obliquely. ("I am always oblique," Mrs. Travers told me in a letter, "feeling for hint and suggestion rather than assertion.")★

She was once asked, she told us, to make up a story of her own to tell at a learned gathering; so she began with the classic fairy-tale situation where the king sets a certain task the hero must accomplish in order to win the hand of the princess and thereby inherit the

72

kingdom after the old king dies. The task in this case was to bring back the smallest dog in the world.

Now it happened that the smallest dog in the world lived under the tongue of a terrible dragon. Many a brave suitor had met his death attacking this dragon directly with sword, lance, or dagger.

But our hero, by some means or other, knew a certain secret: This dragon loved chocolate biscuits—cookies, as we in America would call them. So the intelligent suitor stuffed his back pockets with chocolate biscuits, climbed on his horse, rode straight up to the bellowing monster, and, when he was within sniffing distance, turned around and commenced to ride slowly away.

What was the astonishment of the townspeople when they saw this handsome lad riding toward the castle with a huge dragon following meekly behind, snuffling and slavering, constrained by no visible shackle or leash?

As soon as the strange entourage entered the castle courtyard, the young man dismounted, tossed a chocolate biscuit into the dragon's mouth, and snatched the smallest dog in the world from under its tongue so quickly that the copiously salivating monster never noticed what had happened.

So the hero brought the smallest dog in the world to the king, won the princess, and inherited the kingdom.

Moreover, the dragon continued to follow the prince around like an adoring dog, and the power of the great beast was at his service, because he always carried around in his back pocket—a chocolate biscuit.

After she had told this story at the learned gathering, Mrs. Travers told us, a man came up to her and said with an air of profundity, "I . . . think . . . I . . . understand."

"Oh?" said the storyteller, "And do you understand the chocolate biscuit?"

The scholar, a little nonplused, looking off to one side and then the other, replied after some hesitation, "I . . . *think* . . . so."

Then Mrs. Travers erupted: "The CHOCOLATE BISCUIT was JUST for FUN!!!"

So we tried very hard not to be like this learned object of her ridicule. But the truth was, we still wanted very much to know, What do these fairy tales mean?? It seemed a rather frivolous study for us if they had no intellectual content or esoteric meaning to be unearthed by rigorous analysis. And when, years later, *About the Sleeping Beauty* came out, I, for one, thought to myself: At last, Mrs. Travers is going to come right out and tell us what this story is all about.

There was, indeed, one sentence in the book that made me think I was right. That sentence, in the form of a question, seemed to reveal what she really thought the classic fairy tale of "Briar Rose," or "The Sleeping Beauty," meant. (The sentence is indeed a treasure, but I will save it for later, lest you imagine, as I did, that words alone can satisfy our deep-rooted hunger for meaning.)

Now, still more years later, I realize that *explication de texte* was not at all what P.L. Travers intended to accomplish in this book. The way the book is constructed makes it even more apparent that the language of story itself, the particular sensory details, the movement of the narrative, the complication and resolution, are all part of the action of the story upon the reader, which no abstract explanation, however acute, can replace. It also makes clear that the story itself has many different meanings, all true, according to the stage of life one asks it to illuminate, and according to the level of one's longing at the time—that is, whether one visualizes one's heart's desire as union with the perfect mate, for example, or freedom to be oneself, or union with God—"to be dissolved into something complete and great," as Willa Cather put it—and to put one's powers at the service of That.

The first half of the book is devoted to P.L. Travers' own retelling of the tale, followed by an "Afterword," where I hoped to find at last her exposition of the meaning of the story. The second half of the book, which I felt at first could be dispensed with, gives five other versions of the tale, beginning with the classic version of the Brothers Grimm: *Dornroschen,* or Briar Rose.

Let us turn first to the "Afterword," as I did eagerly when I first read the book all those years ago.

There indeed the author offers many generalizations—observations about the role of fairy tales in her own life, and how the characters and events in them relate to ours. Just as the Thirteen Wise Women at the christening of Princess Rose bestowed upon her every good gift (and one not so good!), some unknown good lady bestowed upon P.L. Travers, she says, "the everlasting gift . . . of love for the fairy tale." For her in her childhood the stories were not at all confined to books. Events and people around her took on the guise and stature of myth. She recognized the Three Fates immediately as her great-aunts, "huge cloudy presences . . . perched watchfully, like crows on a fence, at the edge of our family circle."

"This undifferentiated world is common to all children," she says. "Saint George and King Arthur, under other names, defend the alleyways and crossroads, and Beowulf's Grendel, variously disguised, breathes fire in the vacant lots. . . . For a child this world is infinite. . . . The time is always now and endless and the only way to explain a thing is to say that it cannot be explained."

She herself never lost this view of things. When I asked her how to understand the tales, she asked me in turn which was my favorite. "Rapunzel," I answered. She told me to look around when I was riding on the subway or walking down the street. Then one day I would see a girl and notice (and her voice took on a pondering, penetrating tone): "That girl . . . has hair . . . like Rapunzel."

There came into my inner vision the image of a girl I had seen that very day, unnoticed by my indifferent "conscious" mind but impressed profoundly on some deeper part of me. There she stood amid the hellish stink, roar, steam, and gloom of the subway station, and rippling down her back, seeming to give off light from its own soft depths: an astonishing glory of hip-length hair. The sleeping intelligence of my heart knew, however blind to the fact my head was, that just as Rapunzel let down her hair to draw her beloved up to the level where she dwelt herself, this hair had indeed been let down to us there in that dark place in some sense to save us—as Beatrice was sent down to Virgil in the Inferno to ask, with ineffable courtesy and eyes shining with tears, if he would be so kind as to go and save her dear friend Dante from imminent damnation.

Thus, once again obliquely, P.L. Travers tried to demonstrate how the tales are meant, not to be dissected intellectually, but to be related to the actual, seemingly random, details of our daily lives, endowing them with value and revealing within them an unexpected dimension of significance, beauty, and terror—yes, terror.

"I am glad . . . to have kept my terror whole and thus retained a strong link with the child's things-as-they-are," she says in this "After-word," "where all things relate to one another and all are congruous. . . . This form of thinking, which perhaps should properly be called linking, is the essence of fairy tale."

A mythological figure is like a mathematical formula: A single under-lying shape or form of movement unites a host of apparently unrelated phenomena on many different scales. That was the form of thinking that arose in me when I woke up to the fact that the girl I had seen in the subway that day was a relation both of Rapunzel and of Beatrice.

But where was the terror?

What if Dante had failed to notice Beatrice that day when he first saw her, as I failed to notice the girl in the subway station until Mrs. Travers called her forth from the underground of my memory? What if he had been intent on playing ball (he was only nine years old and she eight) or preoccupied with a problem in arithmetic? What if the terror lies in our not knowing what we're missing? Or worse still, what if it lies in what we—like the protagonist in Henry James' story "The Beast in the Jungle"—in our habitual torpor, *have* missed?

"To be in jeopardy is a proper fairy-tale situation," says P.L. Travers. "Danger is at the heart of the matter, for without danger how shall we foster the rescuing power?" Without the Thirteenth Wise Woman and her curse upon the Princess there would be no story. After the first eleven bestow upon the infant Briar Rose every good gift, in sweeps the Thirteenth. Because the King had only twelve golden plates, she has not been invited to the party. Hence she is possessed by resentment and the lust for revenge—naturally! How well, alas, I know the feeling!

Or should I say alas? What would animate us were it not for the influx of these powerful natural energies? That does not mean we need to be possessed by them, like the Thirteenth Wise Woman. She is a spirit, or force of Nature, and subject to other standards than ourselves.

But maybe there is some way other than murder or suffocation, as the hero of Mrs. Travers' made-up fairy tale knew, for human beings to deal with these terrible, vivifying, monsters in ourselves.

That doesn't mean that her clever hero's way was necessarily easier than head-on battle with the dragon. It must have required enormous intelligence and tenacity to ferret out the dragon's secret weakness, and great courage to ride up unarmed and look the beast in the face. Then, for the rest of his life, in order to have the dragon's power at his command, the prince must have had to be always vigilant, lest the beast run amok, and always prepared with the necessary deterrent at those moments when he noticed that it was starting to grumble *sotto voce,* or was breathing a little faster, or showing other signs of getting ready to lay waste the kingdom. (I am assuming this was not a fire-breathing dragon, else the smallest dog in the world would have been roasted long before the hero could retrieve it.)

Well, as we all know, the Thirteenth Wise Woman says that the Princess Rose will prick her finger with a spindle on her fifteenth birthday and fall down dead. Thus the "bad fairy" fosters the rescuing power, for the Twelfth Wise Woman (who is inclined to be benevolent, having been served her sweetmeats on a golden plate) steps in and says the Princess will not die on that fifteenth birthday but will fall asleep for a hundred years.

And had she not slept for a hundred years—a magical sleep, wherein time could not age her nor corruption come near her—how could she have been there for the True Prince, who wouldn't even be born when she fell asleep but would arrive a hundred years thence to the day? The peril the Thirteenth Wise Woman called down upon the Princess turns out to have been not such a bad thing after all.

So P.L. Travers puts herself in jeopardy—risking the charge of arrogance, she admits—by including, first thing in this book about "The Sleeping Beauty," her own retelling of the tale. Her version of the story, "true to the law of the fairy tale, makes no attempt to explain. One could call it perhaps a meditation, for it broods and ponders upon the theme, elaborating it here and there with no other thought than of bringing out what the writer feels to be further hidden meanings."

Turning back from the "Afterword" to this retelling, we find that indeed the teller elaborates from the first sentence—revealing to us that "once upon a time" is not a time in the past but "a time that never was and is always." Fairyland "intersects our mortal world at every point and at every second."

That I cannot see it does not necessarily imply that it does not exist. Would it not take an acute attentiveness to every second of our mortal experience to perceive it? As for me, it seems I am always thinking of something else. That is how I missed Rapunzel in the subway station.

P.L. Travers continues on her way, telling the timeless story, "elaborating here and there," revealing here and there also, it must be confessed (somewhat to the detriment of men), her not altogether unbiased views of the differences between men and women. It may be, though, that in attributing logic to the Sultan, Rose's father, and her own kind of "brooding and pondering" to the Sultana, she only wished to dramatize the limitations of logic in dealing with the great, feminine powers of Nature. This was the point made in Greek tragedies, and seems to be the point being demonstrated on the stage of history right now. There was something Oedipus did not understand when he set out to solve his problem by logic, and it seems there was something the fathers of science did not understand when they set out in the sixteenth century to "master Nature."

The Sultan, in P.L. Travers' version of the story, senses the danger in the problem of the noncorrespondence between the number of Wise Women and the number of golden plates, but he does not listen to his own intuition. Had he listened to it, he would have been obliged to bestir himself and take quick action to avert the inevitable consequences. He *could* have had another golden plate made, for example, for "numerous sacks of gold" stood in his cellar.

Of course, had he done so, there would have been no story.

In any case, he leaves the matter to chance. Thus, like Oedipus, he himself is really the one responsible for the disaster. Lacking self-knowledge and undervaluing his own more "feminine" forms of perception, he waits until the damage is done and then tries to avert the resulting peril to his daughter by means of logic. If she is to drop dead or fall into a hundred-year sleep on her fifteenth birthday thanks to the prick of a spindle, he will order all the spindles in the kingdom to be destroyed right now, and that will be that. "It is all a question of logic, merely."

But great as logic is, it does not suffice to solve every problem in life. In the present case, it is not a question of logic at all. It is a question of the wrath of one of the great powers of Nature to whom due respect has not been paid.

What if the great powers of Nature *are* animate?

In recent years, when the damage our reductionist view has done to Nature has become all too apparent, many investigators are coming, not so much to the theory as to the *experience* of how, when our constant ego-protective inner chattering and calculating are persuaded to fall silent, Nature can suddenly reveal herself once more as alive.

Here is how Father Thomas Berry describes such a moment of changed perception:

> We need only look at the surrounding universe in its more opaque material aspects—look at it, listen to it, feel and experience the full depths of its being. Suddenly its opaque quality, its resistance, falls away, and we enter into a world of mystery. What seemed so opaque and impenetrable suddenly becomes radiant with intelligibility, powerful beyond imagination. (*The Dream of the Earth.* San Francisco: Sierra Club Books, 1988.)

And, more recently, David Abram:

> Even as I gaze out across the wooded hills, my mind seems muddled . . . by ideas and associations that keep me from directly sensing and responding to the animate earth around me. I try to relax, and so begin to breathe more deeply, enjoying the coolness of the breeze as it floods in at my nostrils, feeling my chest and abdomen slowly expand and contract. My thinking begins to ease, the internal chatter gradually taking on the rhythm of the in-breath and the out-breath, the words themselves beginning to dissolve, flowing out with each exhalation to merge with the silent breathing of the land. The interior monologue dissipates, slowly, into the rustle of pine needles and the stately gait of the clouds. (*The Spell of the Sensuous: Perception and Language in a More-Than-Human World.* New York: Pantheon Books, 1996.)

It is not a matter of "extrasensory perception," but precisely of *sensory* perception. Abram traces out how the introduction of completely phonetic (as opposed to pictographic) written language has been one factor in the falling asleep of this aspect of ourselves. Slowly we ceased to hear the voices of the clouds and trees and began to hear only the voices in the black-and-white marks on the page. When we ceased to perceive meaning in our immediate sensory experience, we ceased to value it. It did not seem important enough to attend to.

This event takes place, not only in history, but at a certain moment in the life of each one of us. P.L. Travers, in *Mary Poppins*, portrayed this moment in the lives of the twins John and Barbara—who have not yet learned to speak human language, and cannot believe they will ever cease to hear and perceive and understand this other language, or that every human being once understood it and then forgot.

Out at the far edges of the Earth, beyond the reach of the kind of language we know, there are still a few—shamans in Siberia, the Kwakiutl in Alaska, peoples we have looked down upon as "primitive"—who speak and understand this other as their first language. Recently, the dire peril we are in has driven some of us to re-approach such people with an attitude of respect, to listen and learn. In *Man, God and Magic* (New York: G.P. Putnam's Sons, 1961), Ivar Lissner, an earlier investigator, lets us hear this language as it is spoken, not by one of us trying to learn it, like the two men above, but by one of those who have never forgotten it:

"Old man forest a little sad today," said the Orochon in his broken Russian.

"Do you think we're going to have bad weather?"

"Shadows linger a little," replied the old man, "creep a little slowly this evening behind branches, trees and under the ground. Evening come very slow. Tomorrow cold."

"Are you going to sleep now?" I asked.

"You go sleep," he said. "I speak little, very little with fire. Fire not so happy today. Fire bad woman, must speak with her a little."

"Can fire speak, then?"

My new friend laughed. "Nothing greater than fire," he said. "Fire very much power, keep evil spirits away, can drive away dangerous spirits, too. Look close. Outside, fire old woman, white hair, many tongues, talk plenty. Inside, fire young heart, red blood, very strong."

"Can you make old fire young?" I asked.

"Put little bear fat in," said the Orochon. "Then fire red like blood and very happy. Fire always hungry. When she eat plenty, then good girl. Never leave her alone. Fire like company. Leave her alone, then she become angry. If no fat and no wood, then perhaps she go walk, then whole forest burn."

"So you speak with fire?"

"Red woman like to talk. Fire here, fire there, like to talk, like to dance. Give me little fat. . . . Red girl laughing!"

The reductionist attitude has the same killing effect on myth as it does upon Nature. *About the Sleeping Beauty* came out in the same year as Bruno Bettelheim's *The Uses of Enchantment*. I cannot help wondering whether P.L. Travers herself—and especially in her writing of *About the Sleeping Beauty*—was not the "rescuing power" called forth by the danger she felt Bettelheim's best-selling book, with its attitude of "nothing but," posed to her beloved fairy tales. For Bettelheim there can be no mystery about the story of a Princess who is the victim of a curse that condemns her to prick her finger on a spindle (which Bettelheim repeatedly calls a distaff!) on her fifteenth birthday and as a result to fall asleep for a hundred years, until her Prince comes to awaken her with a kiss. It is a story of menstruation, no more, no less. The purpose of the hedge of thorns is to protect her from "premature sexual encounters," and its transformation into a yielding hedge of flowers as the right Prince finally approaches implies that she has reached maturity and is ready for sexual intercourse—that is, waking up.

P.L. Travers acknowledges this "strong element of eroticism" in the story. "Indeed, it can be said with truth that every fairy tale that deals with a beautiful heroine and a lordly hero is, *among many other things,* speaking to us of love, laying down patterns and examples for *all our human loving.*" [Emphases mine.] The basic physiological sequence to which Bettelheim confines the meaning of the story applies; but it resounds with overtones on all the levels of love, to which we will be deaf if we fall victim to the withering blight of "nothing but." Mrs. Travers herself wrote an urgent essay that appeared some years ago on the front page of *The New York Times Book Review* asking the readers Please to tell the children of the future—when she herself would no longer be here to tell them—that *nothing is ever nothing but.*

At another stage of a woman's life, for example, the story can take on a meaning opposite to the one in which Bettelheim imprisons it. Doris Lessing, in *The Summer Before the Dark,* implies that a woman in middle age may look back on the first sexual intercourse as a falling asleep rather than a waking up.

> . . . it was seeming to her more and more (because of this sexuality, something displaced, like an organ lifted out of her body and laid by her side to look at, like a deformed child without function or future or purpose) as if she were just coming around from a spell of madness that had lasted all the years since that point in early adolescence when her nature had demanded she must get herself a man (she had put it romantically then of course) until recently, when the drug had begun to wear off. All those years were now seeming like a betrayal of what she really was. While her body, her needs, her emotions—all of herself—had been turning like a sunflower after one man, all that time she had been holding in her hands something else, the something precious, offering it in vain to her husband, to her children, to everyone she knew—but it had never been taken, had not been noticed. But this thing she had offered, without knowing she was doing it, which had been ignored by herself and by everyone else, was what was real in her.

And P.L. Travers tells us in her "Afterword,"

> There are those who see the tale exclusively as a nature myth, as the earth in spring, personified as a maiden, awaking from the long dark sleep of winter; or as a seed hidden deep in the earth until the kiss of the sun makes it send forth leaves. This is undoubtedly an aspect of the story. But a symbol, by the very fact of being a symbol, has not one sole and absolute meaning. It throws out light in every direction. Meaning comes pouring from it.

Now we come to the sentence in the "Afterword" that I carried off with such triumph from my first reading of *About the Sleeping Beauty.* It was as if I had extracted the pearl from the oyster, supposing what was left behind to be of little value:

> What is it in *us* that at a certain moment suddenly falls asleep? Who lies hidden deep within us? And who will come at last to wake us, what aspect of ourselves?
> Are we dealing here with the sleeping soul and all the external affairs of life that hem it in and hide it; something that falls asleep after childhood, something that not to waken would make life meaningless?

This sentence went through me (as Keats said of any glimpse of his beloved Fanny Brawn) "like a spear." When I had read it, I closed the book. And when I went to thank Mrs. Travers for writing the book, I really meant that sentence alone.

But I see now that in my lust for explanations I had overlooked the sentence that follows—the concluding sentence of the "Afterword":

> To give an answer, supposing we had it, would be breaking the law of the fairy tale. And perhaps no answer is necessary. It is enough that we ponder upon and love the story and ask ourselves the question.

What is "the sleeping soul"? The expression stirs something deep in feeling, but the head is hard put to it to come up with any clear definition, the word has been given so many different meanings over the centuries. One has the feeling that it is something feminine in us— that is, receptive—though not confined to women. Thus feminine, receptive sexuality can symbolize it, but is not to be equated with it. Feminine sexuality—all sexuality, in fact—is not individual, as Doris Lessing's heroine awoke to realize (though every neophyte imagines his or her experience to be unique), whereas the soul, as well as being something receptive, has to do with "what is real is us," what is *our own*. In P.L. Travers' retelling of the story, "bringing out what the writer feels to be further hidden meanings," she describes what the Prince experienced when, having climbed the winding stair to the top of the tower and entered the inmost chamber, he saw the sleeping Princess for the first time: "He knew himself to be at the centre of the world and that, in him, all men stood there, gazing at their hearts' desire—or perhaps their inmost selves."

And we know, from our religious education (or lack of it) that the soul is supposed to have something to do with our relation to God, or the Divine, or Sacred, however we understand those words. Father Berry and David Abram suggest that we lost the way to direct experience of the reality to which those words once referred when we lost respect for our immediate sensory experience—the perceptiveness of the sensitive body, as Abram calls it—and lost the way to the inner silence that awareness of such experience requires. Prophetic Shakespeare, who lived at the moment of birth of Western science, foretold this loss in *King*

Lear when he allowed Cordelia, a Princess and the youngest of three daughters, whose name contains the word "heart" or "core" ("What shall Cordelia do? Love and be silent."), *not* to be rescued.

"It is surely not a matter of 'going back,'" as Abram says, "but rather of coming full circle, uniting our capacity for cool reason with those more sensorial and mimetic ways of knowing." "Cool reason" belongs to the heroic ego, but the awakening of immediate sensory perception through inner silence is a doorway to the Sacred.

> All things, all places, are sacraments to which we pay the reverence of complete awareness. With that attention, a universal resonance comes forth from all around us, and this universality, this sense of oneness—glimpsed only through close attention to the present moment, moment after moment—is the simple, great secret of existence. (Peter Matthiessen, "Afterword," in *The Circle of Life: Rituals for the Human Family Album*. HarperSanFrancisco, 1991.)

When she asks whether the Sleeping Beauty might be our sleeping soul, P.L. Travers comes as close as she ever came in her life, to my knowledge, to "explaining" a fairy tale. She places this question at the end of the "Afterword" and follows it immediately with the advice not to answer it, lest we break the law of the fairy tale. Next, as a kind of silent demonstration of what she means, she includes the "latest, and best known, telling of the story," by the Brothers Grimm. As she says, "Over the centuries it has been refined and purged of dross. It is as though the tale itself, through its own energy and need, had winnowed away everything but the true whole grain. . . . Bradly-Birt's stark narrative has been elaborated; Jeremiah Curtin's over-wordiness has been curbed; Basile's gross justification for his gross events—that fortune brings luck to those that sleep—is seen for the graceless thing it is and dropped accordingly; Perrault's sophistries fall away and the story emerges clear, all essence."

By placing it exactly where she has placed it, P.L. Travers has allowed *Dornroschen*, or "Briar Rose," the version of the Brothers Grimm, to speak for itself. If you read this version and then go on to the other four, their coarseness and their ungainly excrescences—the rape of the Princess in her sleep, which Basile considers "luck," the lust of the cannibal mother-in-law to devour the tender babes which the Princess (much to her astonishment) finds in her chamber with her when she wakes up, one of them having sucked the soporific sliver of flax (which in this version replaces the spindle) out of her finger—bring a kind of submarine shock of revulsion to the body, and you hurry back to the version of the Brothers Grimm.

It is like a pebble so smoothed by the currents of time that have flowed over it that it feels as cool and smooth and complete in the palm of the hand as the "little thing the size of a hazelnut, round like a ball," that Christ placed in the palm of Julian of Norwich: "I looked at it thoughtfully and wondered, 'What is this?' And the answer came, 'It is all that is made.'" It shines like the Aleph the man in Jorge Luis Borges' story of that name found under the cellar stairs: "a small iridescent sphere . . . of almost unbearable brilliance [whose] . . . diameter was probably little more than an inch, but all space was there."

Anything that is complete and perfect contains all things. Its greatness does not depend upon its size but on its stillness. Simone Weil said in her *Notebooks,* (Vol. I, p. 32), "When composing a piece of music or poetry you have in view a certain inward silence of the soul and you dispose the sounds or the words in such a way as to render the ardent desire for this silence perceptible to others." The Grimm version, in its perfection, has this effect upon the reader.

I see I have lived through a demonstration of David Abram's thesis. This lust to translate fairy tales into the language of the abstract intellect, under the illusion that when this translation is accomplished we will "understand" the story, is not confined to me, nor to our small group studying the stories with Mrs. Travers so long ago. It seems to be the initial impulse of every "educated" grownup—educated, that is, in the social customs, taboos, and most importantly, the common speech or language of modern Western civilization. I feel it tugging at me still. These sensory details are all very well for decoration, but let us forge on and get to the *meaning* of the story!

But, as in the graphic arts, and indeed in poetry and myth, the meaning of a fairy tale may be *in* the sensory details. What if the same is true of our own lives?

In the end, there is nothing to do but turn to *Dornroschen* in the readily available collection of the Grimms' tales translated by Margaret Hunt (New York: Pantheon Books, 1944) or in this beautiful little book by P.L. Travers (taking care to correct the typographical error on the first page of the story that must have pierced her like a thorn: "golden *places*" should be "golden *plates*." She has placed it in the center of her book like a jewel in its setting. Read it—or better still, ask someone to read it to you aloud. Let it drop into you like a stone.

Then, in the perceptions of your sensitive body, you will heavily experience the falling asleep of the King and Queen, the horses in the stable, the dogs in the yard, the pigeons upon the roof; you will feel the hedge of thorns that grew close up round the sleeping castle pierce your very flesh and you will know, without any words (but with inexplicable sorrow), what it "means."

By the same token, and through the same long-lost and now rediscovered form of perception, you will experience the joy of the waking up: "And the horses in the courtyard stood up and shook themselves; the hounds jumped up and wagged their tails; the pigeons upon the roof pulled out their heads from under their wings, looked around and flew into open country."

So may it be with us all.

---

* She could be assertive enough when she wanted to, as this story she told us demonstrates.

When Walt Disney was making his film of *Mary Poppins,* he invited the author to Hollywood to view the result, even going so far as to meet her at the airport. As they settled into the back seat of the taxi, he stuck out his hand and said, with his ingratiating Mickey Mouse smile, "You can call me Walt."

Pulling herself up into her most formidable posture of Old World dignity, the famous author replied, "*You* can call *me* Mrs. Travers."

"Stick to your guns, lady!" said the cab driver.

(It is for this reason that, within the confines of this essay, I call her Mrs. Travers—I am still trembling!—or P.L. Travers, which was the name she chose to use as an author.)

A GOOD GIFT

Thoughts on *The Fox at the Manger*

by Brian Sibley

I T WAS A GIFT. The first gift, in fact, which P.L. Travers ever gave me. I should explain that the gift was not given *in person*. The year was 1963, and the teenager whom I then was chanced upon a little book in his local book shop. This was long before I met and became friends with Pamela and made a radio dramatization for the BBC of that very book.

What was it that made me pick it up? Not the writer's name, or the prominently displayed announcement that it was by the "Author of MARY POPPINS." In truth, I had yet to read the "Poppins" books; and Walt Disney's film which was to introduce me—like many others —to P.L. Travers' magical nanny, was still a year away from our cinema screens.

No, what caught my eye was Thomas Bewick's intensely-focused engraving of a fox, glimpsed suddenly in the shadow of rocks and over-hanging foliage, looking up from a feast of fresh-caught chicken and staring warily, yet unflinchingly, at me out of the picture. And what caught my imagination was the title in watery blue-green lettering on the dull, dun-colored dust-wrapper: *The Fox at the Manger*. What a bizarre, almost blasphemous, idea: the wild, rough, red-haired chicken-thief at the place where the mysterious drama of the Incarnation had been enacted. My response was, undoubtedly, exactly what the author had sought to achieve.

I parted with the princely sum of ten shillings and sixpence (more than two weeks' pocket money), carried home this slim volume, and read it by the multicolored lights of our family Christmas tree. I read it at a sitting: from the opening—in which the choir of St. Paul's Cathedral "like musical news-boys" fling their glad tidings up into the great dark dome—through to the end, the swan's flight down the Mall in London and across time and space to join the fox at the manger. And when I had finished, I knew that I would treasure the story forever.

That is why I describe the book as being a being a gift from the author. It was exactly that—just as in other years Charles Dickens gave me *A Christmas Carol,* James Thurber handed me a copy of *The Thirteen Clocks,* and Kenneth Grahame made me a present of *The Wind in the Willows.*

After Christmas, I wrapped up my copy of *The Fox at the Manger* and sent it to the author—care of the publishers—with sufficient return postage and a letter asking if the book might be signed. The request was granted and—though many years were to pass before we would correspond again and, eventually, meet—our journey towards friendship had begun. It was "a long way and yet no distance," as Pamela Travers says in the closing paragraphs of *The Fox at the Manger:* "The end of the world is hard to find, but it may be as near as it is far, east of the sun and west of the moon or just around the corner."

In writing now of this little book, it is difficult to divorce the sense of wonder and mystery—of profound wisdom glimpsed but not fully understood—that was mine almost forty years ago, from the way I now view *The Fox at the Manger* in the light of what I came to know about its author and her other writings. If they have no other value, let these thoughts stand as my own small gift to another generation of readers.

The first thing to say about *The Fox at the Manger* is that it was one of two books—the other being *Friend Monkey*—which the author would sometimes admit to being personal favorites among her work. Certainly, the authorial voice is clearly to be heard from the very beginning and the "Author's Note":

This story is based on fact and fancy and the characters are fictitious, but only in the sense that people in fairy tales are fictitious. In the land that lies east of the sun and west of the moon they may perhaps be true. For the facts of that world are the legends of ours.

This playfully argued theory is clearly from a writer with a passion for fairy stories. And fables, too; for the tale which is to follow will quote repeatedly from the various foxy appearances in the moral yarns of Aesop. Pamela Travers had loved such stories since childhood and wove many of their characters and fancies into the tapestry of her own tales—just as Lewis Carroll, Hans Christian Andersen, J.M. Barrie, and C.S. Lewis had done before her. In the *Mary Poppins* books, her own enchanted characters—Mary herself and her magical friends and relations—cohabit with the fanciful folk, talking creatures, and mythological beings of lore and legend.

The "Author's Note" acknowledges her debt to the anonymous storytellers of the world, personified by the popular abbreviation "Anon." In the process, she uses the word as if it were a proper name and so gives a seeming identity to the Unknown. P.L. Travers, in fact, often identified herself with "Anon"—the "begetter of all legends" as she calls him here. She would claim, with a willfulness that was not entirely self-deprecating, that anonymity is the highest accolade to which an author can aspire. "I don't want to invoke any publicity," she told me in a letter written in 1987, "but to live, as I have always done, the life of Anon. (After all, Anon wrote the best poetry!)"

The author's hesitancy about accepting ownership of her creations also finds expression in the dismissive responses of Mary Poppins whenever Jane and Michael Banks question her involvement in their extraordinary adventures, such as the nocturnal outing to the Zoo:

"Mary Poppins," [Jane] said, looking very hard at her, "were you at the Zoo last night?"

Mary Poppins' eyes popped.

"At the Zoo? In the middle of the night? Me? A quiet, orderly person who knows that early to bed, early to rise makes a man healthy, wealthy and wise?"

"But *were* you?" Jane persisted.

"I have all I need of zoos in this nursery, thank you," said Mary Poppins uppishly. "Hyenas, orang-utans, all of you. Sit up straight, and no more nonsense."

On another occasion, Michael asks Jane how Mary Poppins was able to interpret the barks of Miss Lark's dog, Andrew. Jane replies: "I don't know . . . And she'll never, never tell us. I am sure of that . . ." There are, similarly, many unanswered questions in *The Fox at the Manger*. The narrator herself asks what would happen to the world if there were not always, among the sleepers, "somewhere, someone, waking and watchful." But when one of the children asks if the world would then stop spinning, it elicits only the Poppinsesque response: "'Who could answer such a question—certainly not I!' Besides, it was far too cold for questions . . ."

The mystery of authorship and the truth of storytelling is addressed again in *The Fox at the Manger* when the narrator begins telling the story within the story.

Was it true, what I told them? Did I dream it? Where it came from I do not know—does anyone, I wonder?—but I seemed to remember every word, just as if I had heard it . . .

Wherever those two stories came from (the recollection of a children's carol service in post-World War II London and the allegory of the Bethlehem stable), they are skillfully crafted so as to fit fact together with fancy as perfectly as a ring and a gemstone or the lead skeleton and the jigsaw fragments of stained-glass window it holds in place. Together they reveal much about P.L. Travers' thoughts and beliefs, and they reflect themes and notions scattered elsewhere through her work.

There is the writing itself: by turns intimate and conversational and then elusive and allusive. The simple simile of children swooping "like pigeons" down the steps of St. Paul's to the rubble-strewn bomb-site is contrasted with complex imagery as the narrator envisions that place as it was in former times—through the flames of the Fire of London to the age of dinosaurs and beyond to when the world was nothing but elements.

Uncomplicated thoughts of childhood and unquestioning faith are juggled with metaphysical profundity: "Are we here? Are we there? Is it now? Is it then?" But just as when Jane and Michael wonder about the stars on Mrs. Corry's gingerbread ("Are the stars gold paper or is the gold paper stars?"), no answer is forthcoming. But then, P.L. Travers often asked questions and rarely gave answers.

I remember an occasion on which I plagued her with my questions for a radio program I was making about her. Finally she balked and announced, rather waspishly: "Why do you want so many answers! You expect me to have an answer for everything, but I am not an *answerer!*"

Even the fox, who is hardly secretive about his life, has reservations about speaking on some topics—such as love: "Of love, I can say nothing," says this creature who denies being a philosopher, "It is always better not told . . ."

As for the three children in the story, they are clearly drawn with the same pen that created the young members of the Banks family in the *Mary Poppins* books. One of them, for example, confidently informs everyone that St. Paul's Cathedral was built entirely by birds. Then the author (who elsewhere plays with words and names so as to rearrange the "Miss Lark's Andrew" of one book into the "Miss Andrew's Lark" of another) not only supports this idea, she also makes a link with the Bird Woman known to Jane and Michael Banks:

> Wren, he knew was the architect; Francis Bird had made the statue of Queen Anne; he had heard the Bird Woman who used to sit on the steps, crying "Feed the birds! Tuppence a bag!"; and he had been brought up on the fairy tales. It would seem logical to such a one to suppose that linnets and thrushes capable of dropping mill-stones on wicked step-mothers would hardly boggle at building a cathedral.

Though the children in the story are designated only by the letters "X," "Y," and "Z" (letters from the wrong end of the alphabet where few forenames are to be found) they are real child characters, possessing the wide-awake honesty of the innocent. They describe the world exactly as they see it, without need to dissemble or be diplomatic.

Their view of the world is irreverent. They look at a Bishop, for example, and see Wee Willie Winkie in his nightgown. This causes the narrator, in turn, to speculate on "what town of the mind" he might be running through, at what windows crying, tapping at what locks. And this note of irreverence is rightly struck, for it is also to be the tone of the tale which follows.

The narrator readily accepts that the children's behavior in so public a place as a great cathedral might seem inappropriate to some onlookers. However, with sharply honest perception, she observes that "these children didn't even *know* they were in a public place, they had brought their own world with them. It was, so far, the only one they knew. . . ."

Thus, in speaking of what they see, the youngsters display unapologetic frankness. When the carolers blithely sing of "the donkey shaggy and brown," one of the children looks at the carved donkey among the figures at the crib, sees an obvious discrepancy and unhesitatingly broadcasts the fact: "But he's not—he's grey and quite smooth!"

As a result of the children's candor, the storyteller herself begins to see the limitations imposed on our imaginations by the images we create in an attempt to understand the enigmatic. Piercing the holy hush of the cathedral, the children's shrill voices shake the narrator into opening her eyes not only to the artificiality of the anodyne Christmas imagery in the bland faces of the wooden characters around the crib. They also open her to the reality of life written on the faces of those around her: faces "scribbled and veined and netted like the inner side of an elm bark"; faces into which life has bitten with "various strong acids—duty, ardor, anxiety." These are the kind of faces that might, in truth, have witnessed the drama in the stable at Bethlehem.

As Mary Poppins repeatedly invites the children in her care to do, the narrator encourages us to look at things in a way we haven't previously seen them: to view a well-known story from a surprising and unconventional angle, to find a wider vision than the blinkered familiarity that can only breed contempt.

It begins, simply, with the image of a Christmas crib and the figures of the Magi devoid of all the scars of discipline and care. In a profound

observation on the doctrine of redemption, she notes the absence of a
black lamb:

> . . . I dearly wanted a black lamb. For, without him, where are the ninety
> and nine? Flocks, like families, have need of their black sheep—he carries
> their sorrow for them. He is the other side of their whiteness . . .

Then it moves from the crib to the mystical thing of which the crib
is but a symbol. Into the stable which stands at the heart of the Christmas
myth, an outsider is then introduced: a character who has no conventional place in the tableau, an actor who has no known role in the
oft-told drama. A fox.

The fox's tale is concerned with giving. This theme is slyly established in the account of the children first deciding to give to "the poor
children" their unwanted toys (a threadbare lion, a toy bus, and a tail-
less rubber mouse), but then swiftly revising that decision when the
moment of sacrifice actually arrives. The toys are hidden away and the
givers retreat, "their bodies bulging with the ungiven gifts":

> O doves, I thought, with the wisdom of serpents! Faced with a situation
> too difficult to manage, they had calmly, without shame or regret, marched
> straight out if it.

The children ask: "Why weren't there any *wild* animals at the crib?
Haven't *they* got anything to give?" The tale related in response presents an allegory on the *cost* of giving. No judgment is offered in respect
of the children's behavior; their amorality stands uncondemned:
"Nothing breathed from them, either of kindness or ill-will. They had
folded themselves completely away." But what judgment *could* be
offered? "A gift," says the author, "must come from the heart or
nowhere."

In contrast, the behavior of the creatures gathered around the crib—
each of whom has already given a gift to the Child—is closer to that
of grown people capable of experiencing pride in giving and shame in
withholding.

Enter then, the fox: "Picking his way through the spangled fields,
one foot after the other making a faint flower-like imprint in the
frost." The fox comes to give his own gift to the Child, and here is the

mystery that lies at the heart of the story within the story. It is a mystery as deep and perplexing as that born into the world on that first Christmas night: the mystery of unconditional, sacrificial love.

The fox will not only give an unexpected gift, he will give it at great cost to himself. But what possible gift, the other animals ask, could ever be given by a fox? Eventually, at the end of a guessing game of the kind found in many fairy tales, the fox reveals the astonishing answer:

> "What I have for him is mine alone. It will not lessen the value of your gifts."
>
> "Let us judge that for ourselves," brayed the ass. "Just tell us what it is."
>
> The fox looked at them reflectively for a moment. Then he gave a littler shrug.
>
> "My cunning," he said.

In that moment, the accomplished storyteller springs the trap of pure wonderment. Then, to compound the reader's astonishment, the Child— "a shadow in the midst of his own shine"—speaks in acknowledgment:

> "Good!" said a voice from the manger.
>
> Their heads went up as one head. And as though there were but a single mind between them, they turned to the crib and saw that the Child had raised his hand. He was looking at them with clear bright eyes and smiling with great kindness.
>
> "That is a good gift," he said gravely, glancing towards the fox.

The fox has given a gift that, at first sight, seems useless. The ass snorts. Neither he nor the others can understand how a baby could have need of such a thing as cunning. Likewise, the reader also wonders at the giving of such a gift to a person whose life and death will be centered on honesty and truth rather than dissembling and deceit— even though that Child would one day grow to be a Man who would dine with such unlikely associates as sinners and tax-gatherers.

The Child's answer, when it comes, is simple and, at the same time, difficult to fathom: "It is not necessary to understand," He says. "It is only necessary to let it be. Love and let be."

Neither the Child nor the storyteller gives any further hint as to what use the Child might, one day, make of such a gift. It remains as unlikely and inexplicable a mystery as the gift of God Incarnate. A conversation, however, between the fox and the Child, surprisingly reveals that these two have much in common.

Accused of never having learned to serve, the fox replies: "I serve myself. . . . I serve, as man himself serves. I breathe in, I breathe out. What I take in from the air, the earth takes in from me." In later years, when the Child is faced with such tricky accusations, He will be as clear (and as enigmatic) in his response. As the Son of the Father, He too serves himself and his creation.

The stable animals describe the fox as incapable of being tamed, to which he agrees. Indeed, he sees all too clearly that the tame pay a high price (for the sheep, it is the basting dish). Yet, despite railing against collar and cage, the fox *is* eventually tamed—at the moment of giving his gift to the Child. In turn, the Man whom the Child will one day become also submits to being tamed and is, in the process, reviled, beaten, humiliated and, finally, put to death.

Like the Child-Man who will one day treat all people—the ruler and the outcast—as equals, the fox is fiercely independent: "No one bids me go here, go there. The king's candle and the beggar's both shine gold but neither beckons me under a roof. I live in danger, as the halcyon lives that builds her nest on the wave, alone with myself at all times, when the wind rises and the rain comes down . . ."

The fox, in fact, rejoices in his *selfness* (what the other animals assume to be *selfishness*), admitting that he shares nothing: "What is mine, I keep . . . I have or have not, according to fate and season . . ."

The unpredictability of the changing seasons and the unseen twists along the road of fate are well understood by the Child. He knows that while the ass describes him as "young and true and innocent" and, therefore, needing no cunning, He will not always *be* a Child.

Above all, there are no half-measures in the giving of the fox's gift. "Half a thing," he says, "is no use to me." And the Child—Himself an image of wholeness—is quick to defend the fox's gift: "It is good because it is not half a thing. It is whole." The Child—who will ask nothing short of everything of those who would follow Him—explains that the rare gifts given by the kings all come from their plenty; similarly, the gifts offered by the animals cost little or nothing to give.

Though the dove sings her lullaby to the Child, it is "not the end of her singing." Though the cow has loaned its manger, the manger will be eventually be returned to her. Though the ass has carried the Child's mother, his back is not broken. Even the sheep, who has given its coat to keep the child warm, will grow more wool. "All of you," says the Child, "have given me gifts that still remain your own . . . But the fox—"

The fox has given his all. In giving his cunning, he has given his independence, his self-preservation, his very existence. He has sacrificed his aloneness and his solitary and separate character: "To be alone is my nature," he says: ". . . Always myself alone . . . Myself alone, dancing at the edge of the clearing, not for anyone's pleasure but my own."

As for the Child who comes "from beyond the world," He knows that He faces a future in which He also will be alone, however much He might wish otherwise:

> "Stay with me," the Child pleaded. "They give me Christmas welcome now. But some day, when the leaves are green, it will be a different story . . . Let it be you and I together!"

The fox knows that it is an invitation he cannot accept: "That would make two of us. You come, indeed, from beyond the world. Therefore, you know well that what you have to do can only be done by one . . . It is you who are the fox now, alone against the world."

The Child admits to the truth of it: He, too, is alone—but not dancing, like the fox, with the joy of being. He is alone with the coming pain of the future; facing an End that is unthinkable, yet known long before the Beginning:

> "You are right," he whispered. "That is how it must be—alone when the wind rises and the rain comes down."

Or, when the time comes for the Child, Himself, to surrender everything.

In the stable, the fox lies down with the lamb—a *black* lamb—and watches the Child in the manger:

> His yellow eyes were fixed unblinkingly upon the Child and the Child's eyes shone unblinkingly back at him. With a look that seemed to unwind

time the two gazed at each other. What they said in that look no one can tell. They might have lived a lifetime in it—thirty-three years of life, maybe—stretching away from this winter night to a far-off day in spring.

The tale within the tale is finished, and the children—unrepentant over the gifts they chose not to give—happily speculate on what the other wild animals might have taken to the manger: fruits picked by the long-necked giraffe, fish caught by the whale, crumbs gathered by the sparrow, and a lucky feather from the peacock's tail. Then one more gift: a white swan flying along the Mall, heading for the stable that is not on any map but which lies "at the end of the world," where she will join the fox and sing for the Child her first and last song—her swan-song . . .

All then has been told.

I have said that this little book was Pamela Travers' first gift to me. Her second was her signature on the title-page. Her third was a friendship that spanned several years and included a time of working together on a sequel to the film of *Mary Poppins*—to date unmade.

She, who didn't bother with radios or televisions, found it almost as difficult to entrust *The Fox at the Manger* to me as the children in the story found it to relinquish their toys. "How is the Child going to speak? How can you *possibly* give Him a voice? Why don't you call the children X, Y, and Z, as they are the book? I don't want them to be given names, you understand, but how will we know which one's speaking? Does quite so much of the narrative have to go? Couldn't someone just *read* the story? I've read it many times—in cathedrals, too! Does it *have* to be a play . . . ?"

Or, on meeting the composer, David Hewson: "Why do you have to write music? There are plenty of hymns you could use . . ." And on hearing that someone would be narrating her story, as if it were being remembered by the author: "You mean someone is going to play *me*? Well, *who*?"

Eventually, however, I was able to give her back a gift of my own: a dramatic telling of the story (*with* music!) and a cast headed by Alec McCowen as the Fox and Dame Wendy Hiller (whom I was careful to refer to as the "Storyteller" and *not* as "P.L. Travers").

I often think of my friend and of the gifts she gave me. Especially one given only a short time before her death. We were talking, as we often did, of stories and storytelling. I asked her if she thought perhaps another story, maybe one last tale about Mary Poppins, might yet come to her.

"I think it might," she replied slowly. "The other day, I found—on the pavement outside—a *star!*"

"A star?" I repeated, somewhat incredulously.

"Yes," she said softly, "a star. Go and look for it yourself. I very much hope I shall find out where it came from and what it is doing there."

It was dusk when I let myself out of the house and set off down the street in search of that star. The light was failing, but I found it at last, just as Pamela had said: a star shape, faintly but clearly marked in the surface of a paving-stone.

Like Mary Poppins, P. L. Travers saw—and gave others the ability to see—the magical in the commonplace, the extraordinary (and unlikely) in the everyday. She had found a star in a London street and had then given it away.

Rather as Jane and Michael Banks might have done, I found myself wondering about the meaning of that star. Of course, Mary Poppins (who, after all, could see "over the rim of the world") would know the answer; but, as the Banks children were all too aware, she would never, never tell.

A puzzled passer-by looked quizzically at the man staring so intently at what doubtless appeared to be a very *ordinary* paving-stone. I was remembering the words of the old snake, the Hamadryad, on that night of the Full Moon when Mary Poppins took Jane and Michael to the zoo:

> "We are all made of the same stuff . . . The same substance composes us—
> the tree overhead, the stone beneath us, the bird, the beast, the star—we
> are all one, all moving to the same end . . ."

This was a gift of rare beauty and mystery: the paving stone beneath my feet, the bird, the beast (swan and fox, perhaps), and the star—the Morning Star, fallen from the heavens to illuminate all time and space from a rough, cold stable at the world's end.

In the months following her death, I often wished that we had been able to talk more about those stars, both of them: the star of Bethlehem and the one on the pavement near her home. But it was not to be. It remained another of those regrets mercilessly bequeathed to us by death. Until, that is, I again read this little book and found the answer to that and many another trouble. "It is not necessary to understand. It is only necessary to let it be. Love and let be."

It was a final gift.

PART FOUR

THEMES

EXPLORING THE HOMELAND OF MYTH

The *Parabola* Essays

by Ellen Dooling Draper

"THE FARTHER I go, the more I like being here," P.L. Travers stated in a 1979 interview.[1] "But," she went on to say, "that doesn't prevent me from knowing full well that I'm far from home." As we look back over the ninety-seven years of her life and the more than sixty-four years of her work, we realize just how far she traveled. We can appreciate with what lightness of heart and depth of mind she could experience "being here," and we can catch glimpses of her life-long quest to find her way "home."

In the early 1970s, P.L. Travers collaborated with her friend D.M. Dooling to create a new magazine. It would focus on myth, tradition, and story, and explore how these expressions rooted in the past might inform our modern search for the meaning of our lives. The magazine was named *Parabola, The Magazine of Myth and Tradition*. Its inaugural issue, on the theme of "The Hero," was published in 1976. During the next fifteen years, until 1992, Travers (or "PLT" as she was known to its editors) contributed more than forty articles and stories to the journal.

As a member of the editorial staff from 1988 to 1995, I had the opportunity to work with PLT during the last years of D.M. Dooling's life and for two years after her death. I was always struck with the passion of PLT's thought, even when we occasionally had to puzzle over the connections between her formulations and the themes of our issues. Our overseas telephone conversations with her about each article were lively, and we often felt our wrists slapped for our errors in editing.

PLT and I also exchanged letters during the early 1990s. She gave particularly poignant impressions of her feelings about her own mortality, and I began to appreciate how all that she had written led up to her eventual acceptance of her own death.

Directly or indirectly, everything she wrote for *Parabola* addressed a specific theme. She responded to a broad range of themes in the field of myth and story, including "Creation," "Death," "Memory and Forgetting," "The Body," and "Money." Many of these essays were eventually collected as *What the Bee Knows,* published by Aquarian Press in 1989 and Penguin in 1993. The title essay of that volume was written for *Parabola*'s "Earth and Spirit" issue under the title of "What the Bees Know."

In the original essay, PLT focused on the collective knowledge of all the bees as a symbol of primordial wisdom. When the essay was reedited for publication in the Aquarian Press volume, the Bee became singular, an individual cell of a larger knowing. The change into the singular is not all that difficult to accept, as what is really in question is the process of *transmission* between the bee, the hive, and the world at large. "I went and told the hive and it hummed. The news would be spread abroad . . ."

This essay exemplifies PLT's ability to weave together the many and apparently unrelated threads of an idea into one cohesive strand. The article opens with the words "Myth, Symbol, and Tradition" and we immediately ask, "What does this have to do with the theme of Earth and Spirit?" But there is no time to stop and ponder: PLT goes right on to introduce the bees and what they know (or the bee and what it knows), telling us that *that* image brings us directly back to Myth, Symbol, and Tradition!

Even if we are still more perplexed, we cannot but read on. Soon we discover, as PLT said many times, that "thinking is linking" (a term she credited to Alfred R. Orage). Idea after idea unfolds and in unfolding reveals something new about the one that came before it as it points the way to the next: The bee is a symbol of immortality; there is an ancient custom of "listening to the bees" which invites us to listen to our own inner wisdom; in our remembering and our forgetting we discover the cycle of renewal; through all these actions and inactions, the world tree and other mythic symbols serve as reminders. For the period of time it takes to read the article, if we accept her invitation to suspend "the cavortings of the rational mind," we can discover an entirely new world. And where might this world be but somewhere between Earth and Spirit—where myth, symbol, and story act upon us directly!

Another essay which takes the reader on a journey is "The Interviewer," her contribution to *Parabola*'s Spring 1988 issue on "The Creative Response." It begins when a young journalist asks PLT where her ideas and characters came from. First she launches into her habitual defense of her cherished privacy. But faced with the perseverance of his questioning, she suddenly plunges, and as readers we plunge with her, into a wrenching memory from her childhood: It is a stormy evening, and her recently widowed young mother has just gone down to the river, leaving ten-year-old Lyndon (PLT's original name) in charge of the two "little ones." The three huddle under a quilt in front of the fire, and Lyndon tells a story about a magic horse. Her spontaneous tale holds them together until their mother returns, and all dark thoughts of suicide and orphanages are laid to rest.

The emotional impact of this memory has its effect as PLT takes us further, past the remembering and into the questions that have arisen. Thanks to this temporary grounding in the heart, we are freed from the fetters of intellectualism and can encounter, as if for the first time, the meaning of *Unknown:* "our beautiful Anglo-Saxon word, intimate, reverberant, profound, not so much to be understood but stood under while it rains upon us . . ." Then, finally, we hear the word of the article's theme: "With the word 'creative,' when applied to any human endeavor, we stand under a mystery. And from time to time that mystery, as if it were a sun, sends down upon one head or another, a sudden shaft of light . . ." Bathed in the unconscious and warmed by creativity, we emerge from this unusual interview, not with answers written down "in black and white," but with questions. Where *do* ideas come from? What *is* the cause of the cause? Do we create our creations, or are we created by them? Once again, indirectly, PLT has brought us to the soul of the theme.

Particularly during the first fifteen years, when the magazine's editorial direction was guided by D.M. Dooling, most *Parabola* themes were two-sided—involving the kind of duality that invites resolution. The subjects of Death, Exile, Sadness, Addiction, for instance, are apparently negative ones; yet each reveals its opposite, life-affirming side. In her editorial essay for the issue on "Sadness," D.M. Dooling defined that feeling as "the state of seeing truly how things are." She likened it to a landing on a stairway, where one can either go down, into depression and black moods of despair, or up:

> Out of this sadness of seeing . . . can come a need, and a reaching up for that possible relationship between our two worlds that, in giving sense to the one and reality to the other, could reveal to us a new world and our place in it as truly human beings.

PLT's essay on Death, "Fear No More the Heat of the Sun," while unflinchingly facing "the unfaceable," is a celebration of life. She begins by describing the kind of ordinary experience we all have had—a moment of annoyance with the small irritations of practical life. From there, she proceeds to a new vision of the meaning of contradiction and resolution.

We read of how a broken chair leg and a lost blender cap demanding immediate repair and replacement (and undoubtedly interrupting a far more creative and important task), have obliged the author to sally forth into the London streets, preoccupied with all kinds of inner mutterings about the depravity of inanimate objects, "saying No to [her] life." Then, all at once, she finds herself at the gate of Brompton graveyard. The October sunlight and the silence of the trees and marble cut through her discontent, and she is suddenly awash in a flood of childhood scenes of playing in the church cemetery as she and her sisters escaped the drone of Sunday sermons. Through the lens of these memories, she watches Brompton's other living visitors—a pair of lovers, a mother and child, an elderly gentleman. All her interior chatterings are displaced by a new appreciation of the paradox of life and death, and its accompanying questions of Who I am and Why I am here. Then, as she brings us along with her to the realization that our end is in our beginning, and that the high road and the low road are one and the same, the song of a wren and its abrupt taking wing pull her back to the present, to the land of the living and to those newly born. She ends the essay by addressing them and all of us, as fellow participants in the dance of life and death: "Pray for me now and at the hour of my birth. I will do the same for you."

Other *Parabola* themes, like "Androgyny" and "Mirrors," are in themselves two-sided images, an investigation of which requires the reader to think symbolically. PLT's essay "Letter to a Learned Astrologer," is a tour of the paired astrological signs that invites just this kind of thinking. Finally, there are paired themes such as "Earth and Spirit," "Sun and Moon," "The Knight and the Hermit," and "Repetition and Renewal" which either offer explicit contrasts or represent complementary sides of a whole.

Parabola's Fall 1986 theme, for example, gave the opportunity to examine both the historical and personal human experience of "Memory and Forgetting." PLT's exploration of this idea, "Lively Oracles," invites many readings, each of which offers new layers of understanding.

My first impression of this essay is of a brilliant overview of mythology and story. In the first page, we meet the Welsh bard Taliesin, and then, among others, Humpty Dumpty, The Sleeping Beauty, Märlinchen (from Grimm's "The Juniper Tree"), the Goose Girl, Rumpelstiltskin, and Isis and Osiris. The following pages give a breathtaking tour of stories from the *Mahabharata,* the *Ramayana,* Lao Tsu, *The Odyssey,* and Norse and Navajo legends. Then, Taliesin returns "and the end folds into the beginning," where "there is no such word as farewell." As I finish my first reading, I am breathless and intrigued. But . . . who was this "I" who appeared, as witness and participant, in all the stories?

A second reading is called for, to enter into the riddle. Then I discover what I had missed: Parallel to the stories, an individual lifetime unfolds. First there is conception, then the almost remembered time before birth, then birth and childhood. At this point, a shadow appears—first to run about the growing child's morning play, then to shorten and fall under the adult's noontime heel, and finally to lengthen again at sunset and the essay's conclusion. These two readings leave me in a swirl of thoughts trying to sort themselves out: the question of memory and forgetting, no longer a pair of opposites, but a completing cycle of experience; Taliesin, the "soul's remembrancer"; and the progression of that mysterious "I" and its changing shadow.

I read a third time, to let the ideas sift down to where they need to be. This time I stop with PLT when she tells Taliesin to take her no further, as maybe there is nowhere else that needs to be visited; for memory itself appears from both far and near, forever and now.

The essential direction of PLT's writing for *Parabola* was just this kind of exploration of what happens when a pair of opposites meet, and what the possible resolution might be. She often described this process as a triadic relationship, following what G.I. Gurdjieff termed "The Law of Three": At the meeting of two opposing forces, in order for an action to take place, a third force must appear to reconcile the first two. The Bhagavad Gita speaks of these three forces as Motion, Inertia, and Harmony. It says that "there is not an entity, either on the earth or again in heaven among the Shining Ones, that is liberated from these three qualities."[2] Zoroastrian scripture (the Pahlavi texts) describes the threesome on a cosmic scale: ". . . light was above and darkness below, and between those two was open space."[3]

PLT saw the rightful placement of the human being as the mediating force—that which might enter the space between light and darkness. The stage for this important task, she tells us in "The World of the Hero," her article for *Parabola*'s inaugural issue, is the "homeland of myth." Myths, she says, are a way of thinking; we turn to them to discover our own meaning. Not to be tied down to interpretation, analysis, or a single definitive meaning, they have more than that: "They have meaning itself . . . A true symbol has always this multisidedness. It has something to say to all who approach it."

She then goes on to state that the same mythological themes arise in many times and places, indicating that "their proper soil and seeding-place is not in any geographical location but in man himself." Being made up of the tension between opposites such as good and evil, black and white, active and passive, every myth needs its villain, without which the action cannot proceed, and its hero. The hero is the one who is willing to "set out, take the first step, shoulder something" and whose task is to fulfill "the essential mythical requirement: the reinstatement of the fallen world."

The hero is an ordinary mortal, with human feelings and fallibilities. This humanness, PLT tells us, is precisely what enables the hero to serve as "a channel for the gods to come down to men." Later, she goes on to say that this human bridging of the gap is even more than a link between the sacred and the human realms; it creates the conditions for the actual reuniting of the principal opposing forces of the cosmos.

She brings this idea of the human being as reconciler of the ultimate cosmic powers of light and darkness in "Lucifer," her essay on the theme of "Wholeness." Lucifer, speaking to God, asks:

> What is man that, outfacing the two contending forces—your constant yes, my constant no, he should receive—as balm to the wound, as dew to the leaf—the power that reconciles them?

As readers, we may feel humbled by such a large-scale view, or ask in what way it applies to our individual experience. On the level of each man or woman within the scale of everyday life, it is not so clear how these forces will appear. Faced with a choice or a decision, for instance, how can I know what will help, what will bring me down? Is there a clear distinction between "right" and "wrong"?

It is difficult to maintain an objective view of my troubles, so in the darkness of doubt, I forget the existence of light or hope. I tend to believe that this one extreme in which I find myself is the only choice. I forget that its opposite might also be true. PLT tells us, in the "Androgyny" issue's essay "Letter to a Learned Astrologer," how *both* possibilities are universally present and in constant search of each other:

> The South would naturally long for the North and the zenith not be satisfied until it was aligned with the nadir nor the sun content without the dark.

This seems to indicate that I should welcome the dilemma, even though it is an uncomfortable place where I am unresolved, yet seeking resolution. I am stopped, momentarily frozen between opposing pulls, like an iron filing between magnets.

The setting for the Bhagavad Gita is at just such a juncture. Arjuna and his sacred charioteer stop in the dust and crackling tension preceding battle, and the two approaching armies pause in midstep on either side of them. Even all these centuries later, the modern reader cannot but tingle in sympathy to Arjuna's graphic and organic description of how it feels to be in that place:

> Seeing these my kinsmen, O Krishna, arrayed, eager to fight, my limbs fail and my mouth is parched, my body quivers, and my hair stands on end, Gandiva slips from my hand, and my skin burns all over; I am not able to stand, my mind is whirling . . .[4]

PLT was fascinated with this place between. She describes it, as did Arjuna, as a place of unease—where one needs to let go of one's usual knowledge and "be as ready for hell as for Heaven" ("Lively Oracles"). And because it is where the two sides of a whole come together, she also describes it as a place of completeness, of coming home:

> where the vertical pierces the horizontal and North, South, East and West are met . . . only one place, one moment and here, where Heaven and earth conjoin, all things are gathered in. ("What the Bees Know")

This place between is also a place of question. "When does the old year end?" asks a child. "On the first stroke of midnight," he is told. "And the new year—when does it begin?" "On the last stroke of midnight." "Well, then, what happens in between?" ("What the Bees Know"). Unless we are able to adopt a non-linear view, we get lost, either torn between the opposites or taking sides with one of them. PLT's childhood steeping in the Australian aboriginal Dreamtime gave her the needed perspective, which she shares with us in her essay for the "Creation" issue, "The Legacy of the Ancestors."

In this essay, PLT describes the nineteenth-century ethnologist Daisy Bates, who lived for many years with the aborigines, listening to and learning their stories and songs, nursing them, witnessing without shock or judgment rituals that were otherwise abhorrent to her western sensibilities. Then, having earned the title of *Kabbarli*—"Grandmother" —she left them and went back to her own people. In the meantime, that generation of aboriginal culture has disappeared, having to go into hiding as other Europeans trampled across the Songlines. But the Dreamtime is still there, and PLT believes that if we can understand it, it is a gift to us. It tells us of another dimension and another way of relating to the "objective Now." It reminds us that we "become our own ancestors," and it teaches us that "our profane, desacralized life . . . is the seeding ground of the sacred." From this perspective, we can understand that creation is not an *idea* of one time a long time ago, but a *fact* that exists in the ever-recurring moment of here and now.

With this new view of the relationship between beginnings and endings, we can begin to appreciate the complexity of the interaction of opposites and their reconciler. We can see baffling contradictions, energies that are in constant movement. In a confrontation between people, for example, the one who at first appeared to be the motivating force can suddenly change and become the obstacle; or the well-meaning bystander who seeks to mediate, if he or she fails to maintain an impartial role, simply enters the fray and becomes part of the problem. PLT expresses the difficulty in "Green Grow the Rushes," which she wrote for "The Triad" issue:

> In the matter of human affairs, who knows what of affirmation or denial, in story or in life, will bring about the reconciling moment? The forces are constantly changing places.

In nature, PLT goes on to say, the triadic interaction is simpler, acting according to necessity:

> The sun strikes on the glowing river and down to the dark mold beneath, and, as in the measure of a dance, the Three, opposing and relating, perform their cosmic service. Thus from their lawful interchange, the rushes by the bank grow green.

At the end of the 1980s and in the early 1990s, as her health deteriorated and she moved into her nineties, PLT's questioning turned even more inward. "Now Farewell and Hail," her most autobiographical essay, was written for *Parabola*'s "Exile" issue about ten years before her death. In it she describes the different stages of her life in terms of search—from her childhood experience of completeness and being at home, through her adult impression of exile and her quest to belong, to her old age and the feeling of a return toward completeness:

> I am here, now, a lost child found, with that Something Else, that painful riddle, again at work upon me . . . it could be that my lack is, on its obverse side, my treasure, that which calls me back to the sole and living moment.

This theme of movement from lost to found runs through much of PLT's work, from *Friend Monkey* to *Mary Poppins* to *About the Sleeping Beauty*. At a certain moment in many stories, someone or something is lost—discarded, forgotten, banished, enchanted, or in some way removed from the first field of action—while continuing to exist on another plane or level. The action on the original level goes on without them or it for a certain time—until both the one lost and the story itself demand reunification, so that "ever after" can be sounded. In the game of hide and seek, although they start from different places, both the hidden and the seeker strive to reunify their splintered community. PLT suggests in "Unknown Childhood," written for the issue on "Liberation," that "all that is lost is somewhere, [and] whatever is lost is longing for that which has lost it."

During the last years, as she prepared for her own great last step in this world, P.L. Travers began to sense that it was to be a first step into a new world, one where she would be welcomed as a wanderer finally returning home. She ends "Remembering," written for "The Hunter" issue, with the plea that she might be "spied from afar as someone comes running to meet me." The illuminating grace and sense of hope with which she met her death was already glimpsed in "Monte Perdido," her essay written for "The Mountain" issue. Here, Travers bore witness to the coming together of those three precious forces she had sought throughout the years, bringing not a conclusion, but a new beginning:

> I could sense the vibrant brightness behind me as I approached the staircase; and I knew that to find it again I must give myself up to the dark and be ready to face the unknown. As I put my foot on the first stair, a hand reached down and took mine. Help was at hand. I was not alone. So I began to climb.

NOTES

1. Jonathan Cott, *Pipers at the Gates of Dawn: The Wisdom of Children's Literature* (New York: Random House, 1981.)

2. *The Bhagavad Gita: The Lord's Song,* Annie Besant, tr. (Madras: The Theosophical Publishing House, 1970), XVIII: 40.

3. *From The Bible of the World,* Robert O. Ballou, ed. (New York, Viking Press, 1939.)

4. Bhagavad Gita, I:28-30.

WHAT IS THE STORY?

by Paul Jordan-Smith

"WHY DOES Jack's mother give him five beans?" Pamela Travers asked me not long after we had met, while we were still investigating one another's approaches to storytelling.

"I have no idea," I replied. "Does it have to mean anything? In some versions it's three beans, in some versions only one. Any number would satisfy the storyteller and the audience, or no number at all. I don't think the meaning of the story changes substantially because of the number of beans."

PLT, as those of us at *Parabola* Magazine came to know her, smiled benignly at my reply. "Exactly," she said. "Some storytellers I know are trying desperately to attribute ponderous meanings to the most minute details. It would be such a help if you, as a storyteller, could go to them and tell them that it's five beans because five is a number."

We smiled at each other and the mutual investigation was over, for we recognized the kindred spirit in one another. Over the years we occasionally had our differences of view in various particulars of storytelling, but we always had a common understanding that the story matters in its telling, not in the microscopic analysis of its details. We shared the view that stories can be much more than entertainment, and that few stories have only one layer of meaning. What a story means depends a great deal on the time and place of its telling, who is telling it to whom, as well as the several purposes of those present. We shared a delight in the insolubility of the conundrum that two verbally identical stories can mean wildly different things, depending on who tells it and why, while two stories differing enormously in plot and detail can be in essence "the same story."

A few years ago I had the pleasure of studying folklore under Robert A. Georges, a man little known in scholarly circles outside his own field, where he is highly respected. Prof. Georges' particular focus was on storytelling, and since the interests of his many graduate students coincided with that focus, his classes were always full. But woe betide the student who offhandedly referred to a narrative as "the story." That expression acted like a trigger, and we all jumped when the professor's hand slammed down on the table top and he fixed his gimlet eye on the perpetrator. "What is 'the story'?" he would demand. And those of us who had been through that particular set of mills and grindstones would watch the uninitiated one squirm as she or he struggled to defend the use of those words.

What Prof. Georges wanted of us was to question the glib way we took terms like "story" for granted, as if it was clear to everyone what was meant. Again and again he would question us about our so-called understanding. What is "the story"? Is it this printed text in Grimm's Fairy Tales? But that's a translation from the German. So, is the single German version printed there *the story?* Even German editions varied over the years that the book was compiled and revised by the Brothers Grimm—Indeed, there is reason to believe that what they wrote down was not always exactly what they were told. Which was the story? And what of the many variants that have been collected since, in Germany and elsewhere? How can you legitimately refer to a particular version as *the story,* as if that version, collected under very specific circumstances of time and place from one particular storyteller is the only version or even the most legitimate? Why should that version be any more valid than another?

There are more questions: Even if we regard a particular text—that is, the written form of the spoken words—not as the story, but simply as a story, does the printed text capture the whole of the spoken version? And as one asks more and more relevant questions—Who told the story? What did it mean for that narrator at that time? What did it mean to each member of the audience?—the whole idea of "the story" evaporates. We can't discuss "the story" without taking into account myriad tellings.

When a text is printed in a book, it is not even a story, it is the corpse of a story. What lives is the telling and the listening, the singer of tales and the audience, their breathing of a common atmosphere, their various but intimately linked understandings, values, and goals, their shared breathlessness of crises animated and reanimated, things and people and events heard and seen in their minds and hearts. What lives is the story itself. It is not what the words sound like or even what the sentences declare that is important, but what the story means to those who tell and hear it.

PLT, in her essays and retellings as well as in her conversation, goes along with this view. As she wrote in *About the Sleeping Beauty,*

> is it not true that the fairy tale has always been in a continuous process
> of transformation? How else can we account for the widely differing ver-
> sions that turn up in different countries? One cannot say of any of the
> Sleeping Beauties in this book that here is the sole and absolute source,
> if, indeed, such a thing exists.[1]

Or as she asked me once years ago, shortly after I began telling sto-ries on a regular basis, "How can we ever say, 'This is the real story'? The 'real' story is the one that tells the truth. And since the truth is not in us, we have to tell its story over and over in different ways, always looking for the best way, the way that corresponds to our understand-ing, though we may never find it."

Side by side with this observation, we need to place the common experience of storytellers. "That's not the way the story goes," insists the child on my lap, when I dare to change a detail. "Tell it the right way." Silly child, she doesn't know that storytellers are always changing details, either because they're trying to be inventive or just as likely because they've forgotten how they told the story last time. Or is it the storyteller who's silly, forgetting the importance of details to a child who draws wisdom from them as much as from the larger theme? Silly child, or silly storyteller?

There are many kinds of narrator, as the Finnish folklorist Anna-Leena Siikala discovered among storytellers in southern Finland. Some are professional performers who tell stories as a means of displaying themselves and their art. At another extreme are those who find stories too revealing of their private thoughts and feelings, who only tell stories with the greatest reluctance. Between these extremes are other types, one of which she felt includes the true tradition-bearers: the ones who have found the balance between the version handed down to them and the one that expresses their own understanding. Finding such a balance means accepting the dilemma of telling the story "the right way" while knowing that the right way is the one that tells the truth—which may not be the way one told it before. To be faithful to "the story" is to accept to be in this kind of jeopardy which is, as PLT observed in *About the Sleeping Beauty,* "a proper fairy-tale situation. Danger is at the heart of the matter, for without danger how shall we foster the rescuing power?"[2]

Though scholars such as Professor Georges and writers like PLT might have similar views of what constitutes "the story," there are fundamental differences in approach to storytelling as such. The folklorist wants not only to know what stories are told, but also to understand how storytellers practice their art, how storytelling itself relates to the culture and to the individuals telling and listening, what the parameters of stability and change are.

Folklorists today include in their studies not only artifacts, such as the texts of stories, but also the things people do and the way they do them—the customs and practices that we learn and teach in our day-to-day interactions. These customs are regarded as traditional because they are based on existing patterns, and, in the words of Prof. Georges and his colleague Michael Owen Jones, "because they serve as evidence of continuities and consistencies through time and space in human knowledge, thought, belief, and feeling."[3]

Studying stories and storytelling under this rubric is what the folklorist does; what the storyteller does is tell stories. What writers like PLT do is to combine some of the elements used in the scholarly approach with the experience of telling stories. The effort is to sift the meaningful elements in ways that help us read and listen to stories afresh—not as folklore items to be studied at somewhat of a remove, but as the intimate expressions of folk wisdom to be understood and used in life. Such a literary endeavor is not needed in societies in which storytelling is a regularly occurring part of life. But much of western culture is out of touch with the art of oral storytelling. New ways of exploring the wisdom of folktales and myths comes, for us, primarily through such literary and philosophical probing. It is not that we discern "the meaning" of "the story," but rather that this is one way in which stories can become more deeply meaningful for us. More than an intellectual understanding is needed: For stories to be deeply meaningful, feeling must participate.

This is no mere sentimental journey. One may be charmed, amused, excited, and generally entertained by the stage performer of stories, but such enjoyment does not necessarily constitute or lead to a deepening of the understanding. A storyteller's performance style may intrude, and the story becomes a means of personal display. If as a listener I feel that the storyteller "owns" the version she or he is telling, then how can it become part of my understanding? Another storyteller may be shy and awkward, yet so passionately interested in the telling that something meaningful whispers or thunders through anyhow. Nor are such moments incompatible in one and the same person. I have heard a well-known and respected story performer privately tell a tale she had only just discovered, and tell it with uncharacteristically awkward pauses and reachings for memory, corrections, stumblings, and backtrackings, but with a passion that resulted in a profound inward silence after the telling: not from embarrassment, but from the breathless realization that a glimmer of truth had been revealed. That was a real story. Later, when it was polished and tightened and performed on stage, some of the magic of that first telling was lost, replaced by another kind of magic that didn't satisfy the same needs.

Ultimately, all participants, tellers and listeners alike, are responsible for evaluating a story, for telling it over and over in new ways and in new situations, for exploring its many layers of meaning. It is our need for developing our understanding, our yearning for meaning and a true glimpse of the world that decides for us whether the story being told is a real one, one that speaks to the mind and heart. This is what PLT sought through her many essays and retellings. As she well knew, stories do not explain themselves: but they can explain us to ourselves, though always indirectly. "It is their role to say much in little," she wrote in *About the Sleeping Beauty*.

> And not to explain is to set up in the hearer or the reader an inner friction in which one question inevitably leads to another and the answers that come are never conclusions. They never exhaust the meaning.[4]

The living story, like the living beings who tell and hear it, are inconclusive; incomplete beings whose manifold aspects and changeability may be revealed through the story's many dimensions. Raising the question of our being is, ultimately, the story's purpose. How can a final answer be given to an incomplete being? "It is enough," PLT wrote, "that we ponder upon and love the story and ask ourselves the question."[5]

NOTES

1. *About the Sleeping Beauty*. (New York: McGraw-Hill Book Company, 1975)
2. *Ibid*.
3. Georges, Robert A. and Jones, Michael Owen. *Folkloristics. An Introduction*. Bloomington: Indiana University Press, 1955, p. 1.
4. *About the Sleeping Beauty*, p. 61
5. *Ibid*.

A WRITER WORTH HER SALT

In the Editorial Kitchen with Pamela Travers

by Rob Baker

A taste, a hint, a suggestion, a whetting of the appetite is what I long for. I can then cook the meal for myself. Never mind. Better too much than too little. (As Miss Brown-Potter says in *Friend Monkey,* "Much can always be whittled down but little can be done with little.") It is merely my own idiosyncrasy that I prefer the lyric to the epic. Even so, it may be good to keep readers hungry rather than overfeed them.[1]

L IKE ANY WRITER worth her salt, Pamela Travers knew she was not alone in the literary kitchen and cultivated a good relationship with her editors. Her correspondence over the years with the staff of *Parabola,* the magazine where most of her non-Mary Poppins writings first appeared, shows how this mutual attention to nourishment took place, as a lively process for both the writer and her prepublication readers.

In a very real sense, PLT (as she signed herself in most of those letters) considered herself a member of the team whose duty it was to prepare a balanced meal for each theme issue of *Parabola.* A longtime friend of the magazine's founding editor and publisher, D.M. Dooling, she had participated in the early planning discussions for a journal about the importance of story and myth in contemporary life—with subtle indications along the way of the spiritual ideas of a teacher both had known and loved.

From the start, PLT was listed as a "Consulting Editor" for *Parabola;* but more than any other consultant, she was a Contributing Editor as well, offering a story or article for almost every issue. She took both duties seriously—consulting and contributing—and frequently had plenty to say about the menus of the various meals, both before and after they came to the table.

Her own participation as a member of the kitchen team varied: She was never quite content to simply chop vegetables or wash dishes, but on the other hand she never tried to dictate the entire meal. And she took her double role of planning the menu and executing specific dishes with utmost seriousness. She never hesitated to offer her contribution not as a main course, but as a soup or a salad, a side dish, an appetizer, or a dessert. Occasionally she would readily acknowledge that perhaps her contribution might not be part of the main meal at all, but merely a snack.

Occasionally we editors perhaps misjudged some of those PLT dishes, criticizing a salad or appetizer for not being a main course, mistaking a soup for a soufflé ("Too thin, that one. Without her usual *substance.*"). Though deeply disappointed by such rejections, PLT never quit the team, never took her condiments and stormed out of the kitchen with a vow never to participate again.

Perhaps the key to her survival in such crises was the deep sense of relationship she developed over the years with individual members of the *Parabola* team, whom she took care to treat as allies, not enemies or judges. She sought to nourish those relationships, even with editors she never met, sensing that they were somehow essential to her own recipes.

It was especially important to her that each new editor should understand her own philosophy. She felt the articles of *Parabola*—both her own and those by others—should be, like Goldilock's porridge, "just right": neither too bland nor too sweet, not too hot, not too cold.

She used her salt sparingly, insisting on subtlety and obliqueness at all times, especially when we editors professed confusion at her intended offerings. "I have to move indirectly to find my direction," she wrote to one editor, echoing the same opinion later by quoting *Hamlet*: "by indirections find directions out."

Again, "In everything I write, one can read between the lines." Or, "Slyly as usual, I send this. It is very short. Perhaps you will think it too merely suggestive. But I am not a bow and arrow hunter." And "Maybe this is too short, too much mere hint and suggestion. But then what do I ever do but hint and suggest?" Quality was always more important than quantity: "But you are used to my Much in Little pieces. It says what I want to say. I am no chatterer."

Metaphors for the creative process abound in the letters: cooking, hunting, woodworking, bees and beekeeping, and her favorite, the brooding hen, ever mindful of her eggs: "We have to beware of too much Knowing. That is the danger. Knowing rather than understanding. The expert rather than the one that is pondering, brooding, wondering, questioning—the hen sitting on a clutch of eggs."

The same image gets elaborated in her "Endless Story" (of which we'll have more to say later):

> "Ah, metaphors! And what metaphor have you for the hen, the gossip of the farmyard? Cluck, cluck, cluck she goes all day and if there isn't anybody to hear it she cluck, cluck, clucks to herself, foolish bird."
>
> "Not when Chanticleer is beside her. She is then as mute as a stone. And, too, when she is mothering. There is a saying among the folk that the little hen hatches her eggs because her heart listens."
>
> "There's your metaphor, the listening heart."
>
> "Well, all female creatures have it."[2]

The metaphor of inner creativity as the pondering heart ("But Mary kept all these things, and pondered them in her heart." —Luke 2:19) occurred often, in many guises: "The wax is slowly forming in me (I don't think I just let it come) and maybe there will eventually be some honey in the cells." Or, on the suggested theme of "Mirrors": "H'm. That will need to sit under my feathers and see if something will hatch out." Or, again, "But I can never wag a minatory finger to make my point. I have just modestly to hint and suggest and hope the point goes home. I'm an Unknower and have to do a lot of living with a theme before I attempt to write it down, whittling all the time. Gnomic."

PLT always approached each issue in her own unique way; she seldom cozied up to specific suggestions on what she might provide, as one early editor found out quickly: "May I not approach myth from my point of view? Well, I have to. I can't do otherwise. I have to have lived it, and *that* is hard going."

Myth and story were the heart of the menu to her; she was not shy about objecting to the way those staples were served up in *Parabola,* nor to objecting to whole food groups as distracting and inappropriate to the general diet (anthropology, sociology, and psychology were her favorite bugaboos).

For her, myth and story were always grounded in lived experience, not imagination or romance. It is material that is not so much "original" ("As for 'Theft' [a theme issue of *Parabola*], I think that *everybody* thieves. In one way or another. I always doubt the expostulations of those who disagree with me in this.") as basic or *fundamental* (if that distinction can be made, and PLT no doubt would make it):

> Everything we do or make or are has been founded for us in the past—nothing new under the sun. I am now so deep in all this that even on turning a light switch or watching water run from a tap, I stand before a mystery and bow. But then, I did not grow up—or did not live as a child, more truly—with switches or taps. . . . Do we know what work is? Yes, one didn't think it work [back then], cleaning lamps, lighting candles, etc. Just life. To me it is far more wearisome now to have to stand waiting for bus or taxi. And the world of mythology was all about us. No comment made on it, it was like air, one breathed it. And I think I do still. I'm a throwback.

Such experience was always a mystery to her, a mystery to be respected not defined. "All true things are *uncovered,*" she wrote in the same letter.

PLT also insisted that myth as experience is seldom sweet or pretty. Discussing an article-in-process on the Greek Mysteries of Eleusis, she once insisted, "I have lived this for a very long time and my eventual article will be a distillation of a lot of serious, and savage, material. *Parabola* is still too sweet and romantic, and has not faced the fact of the virulence of myth. In a word, it is Romantic. What it lacks is the bone and sinew of Classicism."

She expected her literary colleagues to be as knowledgeable and precise (especially about mythology) as she herself was, but for a reason: "The use of 'not' for 'now' . . . makes nonsense of the whole piece and it grieves me that readers will misunderstand. I don't want people to misunderstand. It's important to me if to no one else." She also resented having her often arcane vocabulary tinkered with: "Dear soul, do not let me be edited, I beg you. When I write 'folkly,' I do not mean 'folksy.' The two words have entirely different values."

PLT's criticisms of *Parabola* were sometimes stern, but never mean-spirited. They were suggestions by a member of the team, not an outsider operating on subjectivity alone, unaware (or uninterested) in the overall intentions. If anything, she seemed to feel she was not consulted enough on theme issues. She signed herself at times "The Consulting Editor Never Consulted," lamenting the distance and isolation she felt by being geographically separated from the rest of us: "I wish I saw you all. It is lonely doing it all alone, not discussing things."

The distance gave her criticisms a powerful objectivity: "My recent impression of *Parabola* is that it tries to make everything too bland, too comprehensible, not to say sweet," she wrote early on, in 1979.

> It makes me wonder what, or who, is the audience that *Parabola* aims at. "Focus" seems to be teaching people—and I do not know what people— things that it assumes they do not know. What childhood is, for instance, and how to evaluate the Dalai Lama. For myself, I had thought that *Parabola* rather aimed at people who have already *some* gold in themselves. But I may well be wrong. It may be that people *have* to be taught. I do not count myself amongst the teachers, however, but as one who is speaking to a brother seeker. Another un-knower, *not necessarily an ignoramus.*

(The last four-word phrase was penned in by hand afterwards, perhaps more as clarification than afterthought.)

The same letter relates this viewpoint of the un-knower to a discussion of Navajo sand paintings by Sam Gill: "When he talks about the foolishness of getting on the roof to look at a sand painting, I felt this was something *Parabola* should truly take to heart. I myself have sat cornerwise while many sand paintings were being made and know that the whole picture is not for me, but only what I can absorb from it obliquely."

Two subjects close to her heart—children and storytelling—were treated by the magazine in theme issues that she found especially lacking:

> I do not feel that *The Child* was at all deeply enough scrutinised. There was nothing of the sorrow, the ultimate "knowing," the serpentine wisdom that a child has. . . . There was nothing in the issue of that in-*nocence* which, in the child, is not only pure angel but also *pure devil;* nor any suggestion of the sorrow of childhood, the burdens it carries and the bitter "knowing" it has in the midst of its unknowing. There were many lovely things, of course; but I felt that the depths of childhood, never again plumbed in later life, were not sounded. Now this is a needle in a beautiful haystack, this comment, but even so I feel I *have* to find the needle.

"As for *Storytelling,*" she continued,

> where were the stories? Was the issue not largely anthropology, sociology and—not *education* which leads forth but rightly does not reveal which *arondissement* it is leading to—but in a sense, *schooling,* which is very different. If one separates children, albeit for the tenderest and most loving reasons, from the slings and arrows of life (from which they are not free in any case), they begin to feel that they are not part of it, have not been given their rightful responsibility for it, and so, in adolescence, they rebel and demand their "rights" and shunt off their grandmothers, even their mothers, to Sun City. . . . Will not somebody take this up from their *own* experience, not books, and, at any rate, ask the question?

Of *Parabola's* retold stories, or Epicycles, she frequently expressed a certain perplexity: "They need a light, delicate, and ironic hand," she suggested at one point. But later she added: "I do not yet understand the idea of Epicycles. I thought they were meant to be short pinpricks to stab the reader's heart and remind him of the main point of the whole issue. But I may be quite wrong." Be that as it may, she didn't hesitate to continue:

> For this is what I think should be implied by the word "re-telling." Anybody can write the narrative of any story, well or not well, it does not matter, it is simply a plain narrative such as children like to hear. But a

Re-telling, surely, should seize the pith of the story and bring that to the eye of the grown-up reader with irony, wit, and inevitability, adding, if necessary, a word or two to point to the meaning, but not adjectivally, to elaborate. . . . *The Arabian Nights* are there for all to read in their own flowing elaborate form. But a re-telling should be like a sword thrust, a quick stroke to the heart.

And again, "Any primer can provide re-tellings. Something—and there are *many* points of view—has to be distilled. Otherwise it is only book-knowledge and does not really become our own."

Her responses to issues were sometimes seen as Monday-morning-quarterbacking by the editors, but that idiom really refers to snap judgment that comes from an outsider. Though PLT spoke always as part of the team, aiming her "needles" gently, their poignant accuracy often still made them "quick strokes to the heart." In the "Music-Sound-Silence" issue, for example, she "missed a fundamental something —a blackbird singing, perhaps. Shakespeare's 'Orpheus with his lute made Trees,' etc."

She advocated, in the end, "Irony, no false hope, wit, deviousness, sex (I don't mean nude ladies), no 'quest for meaning' but rather being found by it, for it is there all the time: this is what I would like to see. Keep the flag flying. No half-mast."

Her criticism was sometimes tempered with praise (at the time of the "Mountain" issue, she wrote, "*Parabola* goes from strength to strength and I am proud to belong to it"), positive suggestions (for contributors or articles, as well as new approaches), and a certain amount of self-criticism ("On re-reading 'Henny-Penny,' I saw, blaming myself, that I could have made it shorter and sharper still.")

Her insights on some of *Parabola*'s interviews cut to the heart of how such conversations should be conducted. "The [Mircea] Eliade was good, but I thought the very good questions came often too quickly to allow him to elaborate on what he was saying." Regarding one, with Tara Tulku, Rinpoche she observed: "The questions were just right, humbly asking, wishing to know, and not just cues for the interviewee's next remark."

She did not hesitate, on occasion, to urge the magazine into controversial directions. She urged us to challenge the political correctness of such things as, for example, the feminist take on the Mother Goddess: "There is no tradition, no myth, no legend, no folklore that deals with Rights. They all refer to a purpose to be served, which, being, served, will set men [*sic*] free from any *need* to ask for 'right.'" She also suggested printing Uncle Remus stories: "Why not use them, from time to time, for God's sake, *not* retold, because each is perfect in itself?"

Yet the needle that she felt obliged to wield on occasion was, like all needles, sharp at both ends; and she often had to remember to wear a thimble to avoid getting pricked herself in the frays. Some of her own articles were rejected, and PLT did not bear such rejections lightly.

Like many canny writers, she couched the cover letters with her submissions with a sly reticence: false humility, some might say, but actually not in the least humble, and fully intentional. "I am always shy of sending a manuscript, always wishing that I had done better," she wrote once, enclosing two. "But here they are. I can only hope." Or again, "I don't know what you will make of this. . . . Don't say yes to it if you don't like it." Meaning just the opposite, of course. Direction by indirection, once again? Winning her editors over to her side by getting them to defend her against her own doubts? Very subtle, but also extremely sly. Just the tactic of the brooding hen to make sure even the ugly duckling egg gets hatched "just right."

Over the years, some half-dozen Travers submissions were turned down by *Parabola*—always with great tact and only after considerable soul-searching. But she was slow to give up on her brood: She kept suggesting two turned-down stories for other issues, quite convincingly bending them to fit the new theme guidelines. After almost a year, she tries again: "You have 'Two Stories' by P.L. Travers, both of which refer, obliquely, without mentioning the word, to *Obstacles.*" And a few months after that, in a parenthetical aside about (again) being the "Consulting Editor (Never consulted, however, and a parabolic, truly lived pair of myths turned down recently!)."

Later rejections also cut to the quick, especially the turn-down of one of her Thade stories: "Ever dear, Doro," she wrote in response to a letter from *Parabola*'s founder. "I was disappointed that the Keats piece was not used and that Thade is thought of as a gimmick. He is a real character. Never mind. Let him go, and of course use Loki [instead]."

Still, there was truce. A collection, *What the Bee Knows,* was in preparation, and PLT let it be known early on that the "censored" pieces would be included. There were grumblings on both sides of the Atlantic over that! In the end, only one of these ("The Endless Story," originally written for "Tradition and Transmission") was included, and three pieces that had been in *Parabola* were, for whatever reason, left out.

But life went on in the kitchen. PLT's submissions came only occasionally after that, partly due to the author's failing health and partly due, no doubt, to a kind of weariness with the process. Even as early as 1988, she was being plagued by some of the problems of aging: arthritis, which made her unable to type her articles, and cataracts.

> Excuse [hand]writing. I must not use my eyes much. And am still feeling the results of the operation. But I *see.* And that is to be blessed.
>
> My piece for *Questions* will be called "Something Else." But I can't work on it, except in my head, for a while yet. So much to do—the two books for the Fall and working with a writer (talking only as yet) for a sequel to the Disney film.[3]

Though insistent on privacy and anonymity (she once removed all references to herself as "Pamela" in an interview with William Irwin Thompson: "Christian names would make the magazine too cozy, too much of a family affair. I substituted P.L. Travers—whoever she may be!"), PLT in her later years began to allow the personal, the Pamela, more and more into her pieces for *Parabola.* She was then writing more openly of her own childhood, her mentors, her deeply felt beliefs.

PLT steadfastly refused to be drawn into editing the material of others: "No , I would not be interested in editing a book of stories. All my work is from a 'natural' and it would be, for me, a waste of energy." She even was opposed to writing an introduction for someone else's book: "Of course I wouldn't write a foreword to it. Nor for any other script. Who am I, anyway, to do such things? I would not want anyone to introduce a book of mine. Or rather, I *think* I wouldn't. I would want it to stand on its own feet." Nonetheless, she showed a keen sensitivity to praising the writing talents of those who edited her (most of whom also occasionally wrote for the magazine). As a writer herself, she knew all too well that the way to an editor's heart is through his (or her) writing-ego. Her praise was never effusive—just enough to win us over to her side as colleagues in the struggle.

There were also the gentle asides about the difficulties and solitude of the task: "Writing is a lonely business in itself. Still lonelier when one is not neighbour over the fence to one's *copains.*" Or: "Keep writing to me, from *Parabola.* I need to feel that there is somebody 'out there' at this moment." And: "You have no idea how much good it does me, how it spurs me on, all alone as I am here, without you all, to have a word flung at me occasionally." It was not just words she missed, but some quite literal tastes her American cohorts could share with her: "Please tell anybody you know who is coming to England to bring me a couple of packets of thin (Oscar somebody) American bacon. It is a' blessing to my boring diet."

One piece of the mystery remains for me, as one of her editors: Why did she refer to me—with some affection and amusement, it always seemed—as a "Bumblebee"? What kind of editor is a bumblebee? What place has a bumblebee in the editorial kitchen? Other than to frighten the other cooks and tasters—which may have a certain purpose and intention.

I've brooded over it "long and long." Bumblebees are bigger and clumsier than honeybees, more gentle and less dangerous than wasps. They make no honey for others (aha! Maybe those compliments about writing talent *were* mere sly subterfuge!). But they do spend a lot of time carrying pollen from flower to flower—and doing it rather noisily, it seems, more so than their quieter and more agile cousins. They present themselves to the world in a costume of black and bright yellow. And, yes, they bumble. It's their way of dealing with the world, of protecting themselves and those they love.

How amazingly on-target she was, from all that distance across the Atlantic. I never made it to Chelsea for tea (in spite of several invitations), so we never encountered each other face-to-face. But in all our other ways of meeting, she managed to needle me to the core with that bumblebee. Maybe any myth-knowledgeable writer worth her salt could have done the same, but I doubt there are many of that species left.

In pondering all this, I'm drawn back to "The Endless Story," that article we at *Parabola* turned down but PLT insisted be included in *What the Bee Knows*. It intrigues me more and more. This is partly, no doubt, because its story-within-a-story stars a bumblebee-like locust, who starts a chain reaction through a whole community with his word-of-mouth revelation of a secret hoard of "corn" that can be accessed only grain-by-grain through the tiniest of openings.

The framing story (also endless) is, on the surface, a fairy tale about the wooing of a princess by the suitor who can tell just such an "endless story." The suitor wins the princess and heads out of town with her; but when he refuses to tell her the "happily-ever-after" of his tale (denying that it exists), she ditches him as soon as they are out of the kingdom limits. Then she sets off on her own journey, soon meeting another man "comely . . . coming from the opposite direction" who becomes her longtime companion.

Their relationship of "living with the contraries" becomes the core of the tale. On rereading the story many times, this theme begins to spread like ripples from a stone dropped into a clear pool of water: The princess and her companion become "something else," larger than themselves as characters—universal man and woman, perhaps, warring and wooing in the eternal battle of the sexes. Man and woman turn into even higher archetypes: the masculine and feminine principles, Purusha and Prakriti (as Travers identifies it elsewhere); and those in turn become the ultimate metaphors of the contradictory but complementary paths of the Mind and the Heart. And what does all this—one of us asked in an editorial meeting—have to do with "Tradition and Transmission"? Or, the current reader might well wonder, with bumblebees?

Yet what other tradition or transmission—or true bumbling—is there than the marriage of knowing and understanding, of Reason and Intuition, that "both ends of the stick, the whole, alone" that is at the core of all stories and storytelling? It is the endless story of self-discovery: The affirming Princess and the denying suitor give way to a mysterious third force who reconciles the original searcher with her self, not through easy answers but through the dynamics of lifelong struggle:

> "You must hate me as much as you love me," he told her. "Only that will suffice."
>
> And she realized that what would suffice for him was to be the order of their days. Whatever might suffice for her would have to adapt itself to that. Furthermore, it came to her, as something felt rather than known, that all is really no better than nothing, that the heart of a woman, entire and undivided, is a heavy burden for a man to carry and that too close is to be too far apart. Only the far can be near.
>
> So, without comment, she accepted both ends of the stick for the sake of the stick itself. The whole, alone, would suffice for her. . . the ultimate goal, the durable fire towards which they went, travelling through the land and their lives, sleeping contentedly by night and by day contentedly wrangling.[4]

She was Rest-harrow, a small pink flower growing in the furrows of newly plowed ground; he was the Milky Way. She was Nature and simplicity; he, Philosophy and complexity. She was the necessary student of his teaching, the understanding of his knowing. She was the dancer in the dance of life; he the cold, analytical onlooker. She was to go on; he, to die, admitting finally the possibility of her point of view: "The mind is not enough. . . . The mind does not suffice. . . . There is something to be said for the heart. It, too, perhaps, has its reasons."

She returns to hearth and homeland, privy to the knowledge that she would now never forget "the concord she had known, nor the fateful meeting with her other self" or that "happily-ever-after," though not to be flatly denied (as the skeptical suitor had done), remains an enigma, a paradox, that comes only (and, of course, therefore impossibly) at the price of hearing the whole endless story through to the end.

We stand in front of that endless story of self-discovery, that treasure, that hoard of golden corn, that recipe for which one ingredient must always remain secret and immanent: the "Something Else" that was Pamela Travers' response to theme of "Questions":

What is it? I have been asking myself that question all my life, ever since I first became aware that after the long aureate day the sun inevitably goes away to the West. And with that going down of the sun would arise the lonely, aching, nostalgic longing that never failed to assail me.

"There must be Something Else!" I would say, not aloud, not to any authoritative ear, for the tongue belonging to that ear, no matter how benignant, would never, I knew, speak the adequate word. . . .

For as I pursued the business of living, the revelries, the moments of tedium, the seekings and findings, I still sustained within myself—though there were times when it slept and dreamed—that homesickness of my childhood. And always—again—at sunset. This moment of the day, I found, has its own peculiar vibration, an invisible hand plucking the strings of an invisible harp. . . .

So it was with my Something Else. What I had envisaged as being beyond the utmost stars is nowhere else but here. My longing has been a homeward journey. *Here* has drawn forth emanations from *There* that reveal the Something Else as my own, my inward treasure, call me to find my place in the world and what it is I must serve, and bid me, as the bee never ceases to gather pollen, not to cease from mental flight.[5]

NOTES

1. All quotes herein not otherwise attributed to articles by P.L. Travers are from correspondence written by her to the editors and other staff members of *Parabola* Magazine, including the author of this article as well as John Loudon, Susan Bergholz, Lorraine Kisly, Lee Ewing, Jeff Zaleski, and Philip Zaleski. With one noted exception, no correspondence to or from *Parabola*'s founding editor and publisher, D.M. Dooling, has been included.

2. "The Endless Story," from P.L. Travers, *What the Bee Knows: Reflections on Myth, Symbol and Story* (Wellingsborough, England: Aquarian Press, 1989), 225.

3. This sequel to the film version *Mary Poppins* was never actually written or filmed, nor did a planned stage version of *Mary Poppins* ever get beyond the discussion stage.

4. "Endless Story," 221–222.

5. "Something Else," *Parabola* XIII:3 (Fall, 1988): 30–32.

JOURNEYER BACK TO
HERE AND NOW

by *Trebbe Johnson*

S UPPOSE WE, her readers, were to go in search of her on her own
terrain: the land of myth and fairy tale. We'd recognize her from a
distance by her sure stride, as if she had traveled this way before.
Frequently, though, she'd stop to listen and look, as if for some wisp of
clue that might be borne on the wind itself. If we were to match her
stride until we caught up to her, would she deign to notice us? It would
depend, no doubt, on what we said. Not: "What destination, madam,
do you seek on this path?" Then she would surely ignore us. But if we
whispered, "Did you, by chance, notice a shadow moving behind that
oak?" then she just might turn to face us. She would not give a direct
answer, but would allude—in a way that implied she knew much more
than she would say—to the behavior of shadows in this place. And then
she might suggest that we sit and wait together to see if the shadow
would emerge again, bearing the gift she perpetually sought: a bit of
the Something Else.

P.L. Travers was a journeyer in the great mythic tradition. As Jason
was born to sail after the Golden Fleece, Hanuman to bring abducted
Sita home, Isis to recover Osiris' fourteen scattered parts, Travers
embarked on the mythic quest as her sacred task. Since the first issue
of *Parabola,* when she defined the hero as one who puts his foot on

the path "not knowing what he may expect from life but in some way feeling in his bones that life expects something from him,"* she sallied forth, year after year, issue after issue, until not long before she died in her nineties, in quest of the treasure that longed to be found. Individually, each essay is a foray into one of the great themes of myth; all together they relate a ceaseless quest back to the place where ordinary human acts mirror extraordinary ones enacted in endless variation by the gods and heroes of many lands. Although Travers is the pilgrim on this quest, we all share the journey.

It is hard to pin Travers' pieces on myth to a specific genre. A few would have no trouble standing up in the category, "Essays." Some are retellings of a myth or fairy tale with certain key moments or motives teased into prominence to fit a given theme. Most of the pieces are a combination of story and essay, featuring Travers as protagonist. She chose this medium because she was "a lover of indirection to find direction out," and great stories, like myths, are vessels that carry their enrapt readers and listeners not *to* a meaning, but *through* the very element of meaning. The story was the most indirect—i.e., the most journey-like—way to bring the deep truths of myth into the human bloodstream. Laurens van der Post expounded on this idea in a conversation she had with him for *Parabola*'s "Dreams and Seeing" issue. "All the most important aspects of thought come from that which is thinking through us," van der Post says. "And this process is the myth . . . [The story] sustains and feeds the human spirit and enables man, and life on earth, to be greater than it could otherwise have been." Thus, the human being enters into partnership with the myth-making process and gains a vital new energy from it.

To attain that kind of partnership with the timeless tales of the ages, Travers approached each of her own stories intuitively, never academically. Although she wrote dozens of essays on the great themes of mythology, we never get the sense that she began a piece with a theory to prove, then set about methodically to do so, organizing facts and references and stacking up footnotes for support. She does not so much discuss her theme as move into it and inhabit it until she and it have come to some kind of understanding. Theme and tale are one and the same: a quest, a land to be searched for treasure.

Like the mythic journeyers who mentor her, she is intrepid; the *Parabola* themes she did not choose to explore are few indeed. She ranges far, but always seems to know what provisions to bring along and, like Perceval, she is able to ask just the right question of her hosts. She knows, too, the kind of etiquette her tale demands, and adapts her own role in it to fit the circumstance. She welcomes help from strangers, an essential trait for a traveler in a foreign land. And because her hosts are heroic men and women from times and lands and tales immemorial, she never worries about proving a point; she lets them do that, with their immortal acts of grieving, weaving, eating, sleeping, and starting all over again when they fail. She never flees from dark forests or demons, but embraces them, trusting that they can help her round out her understanding of the whole. Finally, instead of coming to a conclusion (a destiny whose existence she would probably have denied), she lets the elusive essence she seeks, the "Something Else," find her.

The name Travers gave to the place of myth and wonder where she was continually drawn was the Here and Now, sometimes the Primary World, "the inner country," or (the land where Rumpelstiltskin's name is uttered aloud) "the country where wolf and hare say goodnight to each other." This was that ur-place and ur-time where "the selfsame themes seem to emerge, as though something in the psyche of a race had ripened and produced a fruit that corresponded, not in its form but in its substance, with the fruit of all other races." Travers, like all of us, dwelled there as a child, she reminds us in "Now, Farewell and Hail":

> The Sleeping Beauty awaited her moment within our crowding forest; the Argonauts sallied forth in their long-oared ships in search of the Golden Fleece, and the waves of the sea, if not seen by the eye, resounded when you put a shell to your ear. Tilly Saville, carrying the daily pail of milk, scattered the farmyard cockerels that forever crowed three times for Peter who somewhere, behind a shed, would be weeping; angels squatted on the roof top, ready to take your soul if you died; if there was an oak tree anywhere Bonnie Prince Charlie would be sitting in it; the Three Grey Sisters, from whom Perseus had to steal an eye and a tooth, were in reality my

two great-aunts and one of their aged friends . . . the sound of a shot would tell us that Nimrod was away hunting on the thither side of our mountain; tigers burned brightly in the nearby bush and God ubiquitously worked among us . . .

In the fertile soil of the Here and Now, the place that, like myth itself, never was and always is, grows the great World Tree—its branches brushing the heavens, its roots delving deep into the underworld, human concerns scampering up and down between, like the squirrel Ratatosk in the Norse myths. The Here and Now is the center of cosmic being, site of the world navel, the Omphalos, Mount Olympus, the Rock of Jerusalem, the Kabba, the kiva—one and all. So at home was P.L. Travers in this place and among its citizens that in her tales she could turn to those great themes of psyche and society, those fruits on a fecund tree, and pluck the bud, the bloom, the fruit, or the wintery twig of any culture at any time for guidance and enlightenment.

The phase of the fruit she chose depended, of course, on the subject: "Sadness," "Sleep," "The Knight and the Hermit," "Money," "Holy War." But it is something more ineffable than a given theme that draws her back again and again to the Here and Now. The real object of her quest is the Something Else, that treasure she has never known and has yearned for all her life. It is the source of the myths and the truth children live by. As a young girl, she felt its absence most acutely when the sun went down. As an old woman, in one of the last essays she wrote (for *Parabola*'s "Hunter" issue), she is as far from and as close to it as she ever was; we can almost hear her cry, "the sun goes down in myself and I am lost in the twilight." She wrote about it repeatedly. In the "Hunter" issue she suggests it was the essential self she quested for. In "The Body," and elsewhere, she calls it the Unknowing, "a particular process of cognition that . . . will take us down to the very deeps of knowing." Writing about "The Hero," she calls the prize sought by that archetypal quester "a treasure that was lost and has to be found, his own self, his identity." In the "Questions" issue, she abandons the effort to define the indefinable and simply explores it:

> It was not more of what I had that I looked for. . . . No. It was something totally other, another kind of world, perhaps, another way of being.

The word "transcendent" might have fitted my need, could I have understood it. As it was, a knowing beyond my knowing evoked the equivocal question that neither expected nor asked for an answer. I knew it was something that had to be borne—or endured—not verbally responded to.

By any name, this elusive and beautiful Something Else is not indifferent to its pursuer. "The quest from the very beginning has had as its aim the knight's self-transformation," she declares. Only when knight and quest have found and embraced each other can each be complete. Knowing this, Travers, the journeyer, is in a constant state of anticipation, expecting the moment when she will be found. "Something is going to be told me," she thinks, sitting in Chartres Cathedral. That eagerness runs like an underground stream beneath all her stories.

A sweet morsel of the Something Else can come from anywhere, since Travers moves in the company of those who embody it. Her helpful guides, essential to all the great myths, appear to her in the Underworld, at the door of a ruined hermitage, in the Tarot deck, in countless other settings, and each provides a vital piece to the riddle that draws our heroine on and on, ever deeper into the mystery. Sometimes the encounter is direct and personal. For example, determined to awaken the great Sleepers of myth—King Arthur, St. George, Psyche, Endymion, Ishtar, and Sleeping Beauty—and beg them to return to a world that sorely needs their attention, she makes a pilgrimage to Glastonbury Tor and there meets Merlin, himself a prisoner of the entrancing Nimue. Merlin reminds her that it is humanity, herself included, not the heroes of myth, who must awaken and attend to the needs of the world. In another tale, she visits with the Hanged Man of the Tarot, blissful now that his card is reversed and he is "foot-fast to the celestial root"; he tells her of his moment of enlightenment, when his head-heavy, intellectual world turned upside down and he became a man of the Tao, determined to "decrease" daily.

Often, it is not one character who informs her story, but a whole company of them with some essential experience in common, gathered like guests at a feast. In "The Black Sheep," published in *The New York Times* in 1965, her laud for what Gerard Manley Hopkins calls "All things counter, original, spare, strange," she introduces us in quick succession to: Esau, the Prodigal Son, Peter Rabbit, "my Uncle Cecil and Major Battle," the sparrow who killed Cock Robin, Satan, Blake's Black Boy, and the Wicked Fairy in Sleeping Beauty, all necessary dragons of the outer world who make it "easier to contemplate the ones within oneself." In "Lively Oracles," she traces the significant rites of passage in a life by marking their correspondence to the lives of mythic beings. In such stories, her intention is not to run up a list of these figures to support a thesis, but to identify with them personally ("I was with Isis . . . searching the land for [Osiris'] scattered parts. . . . I followed in Demeter's footsteps. . . . I was there when Odin hung on the Tree" and, when necessary, to defend them against those who would misunderstand ("'You love the Wicked Fairy?' said my parents, raising their eyebrows at each other").

In the way of myth, some of her wisest guides are seemingly simple people who have not forgotten what obeisances must be performed to stay in good stead in the Here and Now. In "What the Bee Knows," it is an Irish gardener who gives her the sacred task of informing the bees, symbol of life as immortality, of the latest news in the community. A favorite character who appears in several stories is Thade, an Irish "Teller, as well as a hedger and ditcher . . . all untutored, illiterate when it comes to reading the papers, super-literate in the matter of ancient lore . . ." Thade teaches Travers how to encourage blessings to flow from Above to Below through the branches of the Tree of Life, explains why God was compelled to invent Sunday, and discusses with her the risks entailed in taking a meal in the Underworld. Travers plays the innocent when she is in Thade's company, eagerly garnering an old wisdom close to its roots.

To attend so personally to the fruits that bloom in the mythmaking process, Travers often features herself as hero of the tales. However, one would never call any of her stories a "personal essay," that contemporary genre that typically portrays the writer as a sensitive soul whose fingers, groping for meaning in life, still tremble from smacks they got when they were small. No, "Myth, by design, makes it clear that we are meant to be something more than our own personal history," Travers declares. So, with every story, she becomes as one of the athletes who bear the Olympic torch on one brief span of its long journey, a carrier of the great themes, questions, and turning points that have lit the way of the world's people from time immemorial. In her essay on "The Hero," she proposes that the hero is "one who is willing to set out, take the first step, shoulder something." She, the storyteller, shoulders the myths themselves. This is nothing less than a sacred task.

Hence, it is almost impossible to stitch from the fragments we're given any sort of autobiography. Travers presents herself as an ageless, often sexless journeyer. It is as if she were determined to make her own history, like the myths, a tale that never happened and always is. She plays the role of her heroic self, greater than life. A shape-shifter, she could take on any persona to get the tale told right. In "Well, Shoot Me," she is the elder who recognizes that, just as the mythic king had to be ritually slain each spring that crops, culture, and spirit might bloom afresh, so must each young generation "slay" the old ones it will replace. In "Unknown Childhood," she decides, after some deliberation, to take on the role of the Dwarf, that archetypal aide to lost pilgrims. In "Speak, Lord," she is the determined quester alone on her path, interrupted and enlightened by Merlin, the quintessential teacher, while with Thade she assumes the Socratic role, eliciting from her companion universal truths that he, in his earthy simplicity, takes for common knowledge.

One of her favorite archetypes is the Youngest Brother. The Youngest Brother is simple and innocent, therefore blessed. He is humble enough to take the advice of frogs and dwarfs, and will never refuse water to a poor old woman met upon a narrow path. Because he goes in search of the truth, he neither cowers from it nor wields it over others. There is a bit of the Youngest Brother in most of Travers' personae—purehearted, expecting adventure everywhere and so encountering it, "harkening to the oracles, following after the way-showers," whether magician, ditcher, or the archfiend Lucifer himself.

"There is nothing that is not made use of," Lucifer rails at God. "And you, Artificer, had need of me . . . so that you should have a nether pole, a necessary antagonist, to sustain your creation's tension." The words of this most formidable fallen angel reflect one of Travers' primary concerns: that the dark and ugly side of a story get equal play with the bright. The dark side is essential; it brings out the fullness of the light and drops upon our consciousness the shadow of forgetting we need to remember anew. We are reminded so by those primary tales, the nursery rhymes. Even as the bough lulls the baby rock-a-bye, it is bending to the breaking point. No one can fix Humpty Dumpty, and Little Tommy Tucker has to sing for his supper. The dark ones of myth "awoke the virtues, imposed the conflict and, by strictly throwing the story forward, brought it to its strict end—the achievement of Happy Ever After." One of the few subjects that make Travers prickle is Hans Christian Andersen, who refused to confront shadow, "curdled the feelings with bane-and-honey and undermined the vitality by his endless appeal for pity."

Everything has its shadow: Death chases love; virtue must turn around and confront pride; memory is trailed by the long veil of forgetting. The pleasurable act of eating can consign us to the Underworld, as Persephone and anyone who has ever made the mistake of "sipping a sup" with the fairies discover all too late. Even the story, beloved entity in Travers' universe, can have its dark side, as she realizes in "The Legacy of the Ancestors." Rescued from obscurity and preserved in books, it is more accessible to more people, but it also loses some of the magic and power it possessed when people told it aloud.

If light curves gently into dark, the bloom into the sere twig, the reverse is also true. In one of her most autobiographical essays, the "Interviewer" of the title asks Travers, the Famous Author, a question that catapults her back into a memory of how her own creativity was sparked. On a stormy day shortly after her father died, fear for her mother's state of mind and for the safety of herself and her young sisters prompted her to gather "the little ones" close and spin for them, out of the very fabric of her fear, a story of a magic horse with sparks of light flashing from his hooves and room on his back to carry them all to a shining land.

For Travers, the shadow was essential for another reason. It was in its presence that she yearned most keenly for the Something Else. This is the great paradox that threads through her work: We must suffer the pain of forgetting the Here and Now in order to remember and return to it again. For wondrous though the landscape is, enlightened though the company, it is no easy task to dwell in that enchanted land and so, repeatedly, we turn away. The process begins in childhood. The growing influence of that cold virtue, common sense, sees to it, as do the remonstrations of adults that God absolutely can not, no, never, be glimpsed in a golden sunflower. The sun and rain themselves conspire to make us turn our back upon their secret faces and ceremonial garb, for they will grow us up whether we wish it or not. Our own humanity overpowers what is great and eternal in us and tugs us toward more temporal promises. It has happened to the best: Gilgamesh struggles to stay awake for six days and seven nights—and fails; Eve plucks the fruit she has been warned not to touch; Orpheus cannot help but look over his shoulder to see if Eurydice is really following.

Such an eclipse of the mythic consciousness befalls us all, sometimes for moments at a time; sometimes, sadly, for most of our adulthood. Even Travers' heroic persona is thrust out of her secret homeland. She, too, forgets to pay attention. She, too, finds that holding on to the gift of absolute presence in the Here and Now is simply too much to bear. As she cries to the Sun, her benefactor, in "The Unsleeping Eye: A Fairy Tale": "Whatever it is you have given me, I cannot carry it any longer. I must throw it away." So our storyteller, who has so long stood under the canopy of mystery in expectation that something wonderful will be revealed—she too slips away into the tempting world of Tomorrow "which would give us everything we needed—importance, relevance, power, pleasure, every ultimate satisfaction." This is the world of the Sun's contrary, the unnaturally illuminated place of "I want, I want" and "More! More!" (Most of us know it well.)

Then comes the real choice: Once we realize we're standing outside the Here and Now, will we try to get back? And how? The question haunted Travers more and more as she got older, when every essay she wrote for *Parabola* somehow bent to it, like the sunflower that ever turns its face to the sun. Travers, the mythic hero, is one of the lucky ones. She finds her way home. In the midst of the mad dance of More! More! she feels "the long setting of the sun" within her and pauses. "And out, from under the leaves of Eden, I rose and was awake, awake and in my lost domain." In another version of the reawakening, ("Unsleeping Eye") the Princess of the tale only threatens to throw away the precious, weighty gift of the Sun, as if to test herself and him. She knows well that the Happy Ever After cannot be achieved without suffering.

Indeed, it takes work to abide in the Here and Now. Using a phrase coined by James Hillman, Travers urges us to "re-story" ourselves as adults, to "relive intentionally what once was organically lived by the blood." One way to do this is to read the great myths. But living them, or letting them live through us, is harder and far more crucial. In "The Unsleeping Eye," a child comes up with an idea for how to begin the task: build a ladder back to the Sun. Yes! Travers exults, we must climb up through the length of ourselves, "on each rung repairing what had been—the wrong roads taken, the forgettings, the long stretches of nothingness—and preparing what was to come." Finally, arriving back in the land that longs for our company, we need to be very vigilant. "If man has within him the potential, if only as a germ, to share in the consciousness of the universe, even to glimpse at moments certain aspects of the Unknown (behold, I show you a mystery!) above all, to learn to know himself, can this be done without attention?" (*Parabola* "Attention" issue)

So the mindful journeyer, willing to suffer the pain of being greater than her ordinary human self, stumbles back to her lost domain (always, Travers asserts, "my longing has been a homeward journey," (*Parabola* "Questions" issue)—only to be lured away again. And then, again, as it must do, the sun sets, and again she feels the longing that hastens her return. The path, no matter where we stand on it, circles round and round in an endless loop.

> I shall not stay long with you, my homeland. I shall fall away again and again, drawn by the magnet of Tomorrow and the treacherous hope that it exists, and carries gifts and surcease from care. Sages and seers, Now, dwell in your pavilions. To such as I it is given only to visit them from time to time and know that I have slept—slept and forgotten my meaning.

Quest after question, mystery after mystery, Travers sets her feet on the path and strides boldly into the Here and Now, drawn by the Something Else that we, her readers invariably discover whenever we journey in her company.

★ Unless otherwise noted, all quotations are from *What the Bee Knows: Reflections on Myth, Symbol and Story*. *Parabola* stories not collected in that book are indicated by the theme of the issue.

MARY POPPINS AS A ZEN MONK

by Feenie Ziner

THE FIRST TIME I met P.L. Travers was at a ceremony at the New York Public Library's Donnell Branch at which she donated a collection of her personal memorabilia to the newly reopened Central Children's Room. The way I came to attend this ceremony is a story in itself.

At that time I was teaching two courses at the New School for Social Research. One was in the Contemporary Novel and the other was in Classics of Children's Literature. We were doing *On the Road* in the novel course concurrently with *Mary Poppins,* which I taught three hours later. Inspired by my friend and literary agent, Mavis McIntosh, I had begun to read a little Zen. So naturally, the moment Mary Poppins blew in the door I recognized who she really was: a Zen monk.

Most of my students greeted my suggestion with disbelief if not derision, but one young woman decided to take the question on. Naturally, she came to the same conclusion as I.

I was pretty full of my little academic triumph, when, on entering Grand Central Station for the train ride home to Dobbs Ferry, I passed the Oyster Bar, and longed with all my heart for an oyster stew. But of course, there was no time. I had to get home. So I went to my waiting train and sat down.

Suddenly the lights went out. The conductor appeared and announced an hour and a half delay because of a wreck farther up on the Hudson River Line.

Since no one had been injured, I could rejoice. Fate itself, was rewarding me.

I made straight for the Oyster Bar. It was almost empty. I sat down at the counter next to a lady with beautiful hands, and before long we were talking. It turned out she was Pura Belpré, the Spanish-language specialist for the New York Public Library—and I had read her book, *Santiago,* to my children's literature class that very day. When she said she was on her way to a reception for Pamela Travers at the Donnell Library at 52nd Street, I was convinced that it would be dangerous, even sacrilegious, to ignore such an unmistakable series of signals!

"I'll go with you! We'll share a cab!" I cried.

"Great!" she replied.

As we made our way to the library, I tried to imagine what P.L. Travers might look like. I was not thinking of Julie Andrews. Those who know Mary Poppins only in technicolor have never met the real Mary Poppins. As economical as a Japanese black-and-white, she is no waster of words, no triller of songs. She is an arbitrary and spontaneous individual who *never* explains anything—but who comprehends form and fitness, who is self-contained, fiercely independent, unpredictable, the very essence of the creative spirit. In fact, she is the embodiment of Zen.

When, standing in the storytelling room, the real P.L. Travers became manifest, I was not the only one who was startled. Sixtyish and square, wearing a quantity of silver bracelets and a beautiful necklace of jade, she was engaged in a ceremonial autographing for half a dozen well-groomed boys and girls—all of whom looked as if they had been made abundantly aware of the historic nature of this Moment in Their Lives. Mrs. Travers sought, and found, a folding chair and sat upon it, so that she was eye to eye with the children. The adults who were beginning to drift into the room held back, reverent. Mrs. Travers signed the books and smiled, about as cozy as a Chinese lion.

And then she was sitting all alone.

"No one is talking to her!" one of the hostesses exclaimed in panic. I, too, hesitated in the shelter of the door before I walked up to Mrs. Travers and introduced myself. "One of my students," I told her, "has written a paper in which she describes Mary Poppins as a Zen monk. Would you care to comment on that?"

The gray head reared, the eyes narrowed. "That is a very interesting idea. I should like very much to read that paper. Of course," she added quickly, "I shall not comment upon it, nor return it. Would you send it in care of my publisher?"

I was dismissed, and a hundred people reverently took their seats.

"Somebody," she said, surveying the group now gathered before her, "has just suggested to me that Mary Poppins is, in reality, a Zen monk!"

Hilarity ensued. But she held up her hand in reproach. "That is not as funny as you might think!" she said, severely. "A Zen priest with whom I studied told me that Mary Poppins was full of Zen, that in every Zen story there is always a single object which contains a secret. Sometimes the secret is revealed, sometimes not, but it is always present."

Turning to the objects on the table beside her, she said that some of these things had found their way into her stories. They had little or no financial value, but they had meant a great deal to her—like spools of thread, wound round with long association. And it was her thought that, in giving this little collection to the library, they would "remain together, after I am dead." Her detachment was formidable.

For a long moment, she looked down at the treasures of her lifetime. A plastic Pegasus. A jointed wooden doll, quite without clothing. A flowered ceramic cat. A setting hen of translucent blue glass. I could see her in a richly detailed but solitary room, pausing as she passed a sideboard to pick up the cat, smooth it, impart to it some of the luster of the mind that would give it a life no less powerful for being ephemeral.

The audience settled in when she spoke of her father whose prerogative it had been, when she was a child, to bestow a name upon each of her dolls. She told of once having left a pair of rag dolls ("Lord Nelson and Lady Hamilton") outdoors in the rain, and of having to confess her misdeed to her father. He had responded by ordering her to set them before the fire "at once, before they caught their death of cold." Her father filled the library with his comfortable presence as she continued:

"When I was doing the film with George Disney," she said, "—that is his name, isn't it? George? [Mary Poppins sniffing at the American upstart]—he kept insisting on a love affair between Mary Poppins and Bert. I had a terrible time with him. Bert loved her all right, but the real opposite party to Mary Poppins was . . . Mr. Banks! Mr. Banks, whose governess never let him touch her precious possessions when he was a little boy. Why, Mary Poppins always let the children touch things. She knew that opening a box was more important than whatever was in it. . . ."

Mrs. Travers lifted the little blue hen from its little blue nest. "I've a large collection of hens," she said, "but this one does not have an egg underneath. I simply could not spare one."

She displayed the little winged horse, a prize she had won at a shooting gallery in Tunbridge Wells: "Not for hitting the target but for *not* hitting the proprietor." Of the Staffordshire lion: "*You* had him listed as a *dog*," she said, glaring at the chief librarian. The one-legged doll, naked and loose jointed, was like enough to the model of Mary Poppins she had found for her illustrator, Mary Shepard, to suggest the lost original.

Then she picked up a small glass paperweight: not the one with the imprisoned snowstorm that was used in the film, but a more modest dome with a house inside, and the legend "Home Sweet Home." "Some day," she said, "I might write a story about this paperweight, because nowadays there are so few people, so few who have that sense of home—a safe place, eternal, hidden in their hearts."

She gazed deeply into the glass, long enough for people to begin to wonder if she had come to the end of her speech. Standing in front of the room, she was sinking out of sight. Could she not go on? Was she about to cry? She seemed poised "on that tenth of an inch difference by which heaven and earth are set apart." Then, slowly, her face lifted toward the light, as if an arrow had been released from deep within

her. Transfigured with joy, she said, "Maybe I'm writing it right now!"
Before our eyes: *satori*.

"And last, here is an original drawing of Mary Shepard's from *Mary
Poppins from A–Z*. She said I might choose one." Riffling through a
copy of this short and highly cerebral book, she looked up at the librarians and asked, "Does N come before L?"

Then she began to read aloud.

"N is for Nursery, Naturally . . . " Her voice grew soft, and softer
still, till she came to the lines "Nobody Notices Night Is Near. Their
heads are Nodding on their Necks. Nid-Nod, Nid-Nod. The
Nightingale sings a Note in the park. The New moon rises, but No
one sees. Within the Nursery, Nothing stirs. 'Number Seventeen,' say
the Neighbors, "is Nice and quiet tonight.'"

And so it was over, the woman in love with the dream, with stars, with
night, with childhood. "Now," she says, "these things that were mine,
that were important to me, belong to you." Her simplicity is heartbreaking. "Maybe *Mary Poppins is* a Zen story. Maybe Mary Poppins
was really a Zen monk. Who is to say? Who is to say?"

PART FIVE

CONVERSATIONS, LECTURES, INTERVIEWS

THE FIRST STORYTELLERS

Excerpts from a Conversation

Laurens van der Post and P.L. Travers

IN THE FALL of 1996, we asked Sir Laurens van der Post to write a preface for this volume. He declined with great courtesy, saying that he could not possibly write anything else except what was already on his table "with a pile of deadlines on it." He did, however, agree to speak with us, saying that we could transcribe and edit what was said into what he hoped would be "a fairly decent preface." Unfortunately, before we were able to arrange a suitable time to meet with him, he became too ill to see us, and it was with great regret that we learned of his death on December 15, 1996.

Sir Laurens and P.L. Travers had been friends for many years. To get some impression of the connections between them, we turned to the conversation they had in *Parabola*'s issue on "Dreams and Seeing." In this exchange, one can catch glimpses of their shared reverence for story and for what it represents to the human spirit. Their two life journeys had brought them a long way—he from an African childhood rich in impressions of the Bushman tradition, she from an Australian childhood equally influenced by the ancient culture of the Aborigines—to spend their final years within just a few miles of each other, in the Chelsea section of London. It was here that they sat down together in the Fall of 1981 to speak about what will happen to the earth's traditions as modern life threatens to destroy them.

They began speaking about the specific threat to third-world countries, but almost immediately their interchange began to apply to all of
us and to the place that stories hold in each of our lives. The following pages are excerpts from their conversation:

• • •

P.L. TRAVERS: Let us go back to the beginning of things. I have long
carried this question—Where, having come so far, will all the stories
go? What will happen to the ancient lore?

LAURENS VAN DER POST: I love the stories because it seems to me
that without them, human beings wouldn't be here. Couldn't be.
Human beings *are* a story; they are living a story and anyone open
to this story is living a part—perhaps all—of themselves. . . .

The very profound process [of myth] cannot come from anywhere
but out of life itself. It is something that falls into us. I have been
very much concerned about this because, only recently, I was asked
to say something about Descartes' famous statement—"I think, therefore I am." *There,* it seems to me, is the beginning of the fatal hubris
of our time. Of course, there is an area in which we think—who
could deny it?—but, really, all the most important aspects of thought
come from that which is thinking through us. And this process is the
myth, one of the most profound things of life; it is creation itself,
which becomes accessible and, in part, energizes and gives, of its own
accord, a sense of direction to the human creature. It is something
with which—if we use our brains and imagination—we are in partnership. [This is the] area from which the myth arises, which sustains
and feeds the human spirit and enables the human being, and life on
earth, to be greater than it could otherwise have been. . . .

(They spoke more about myth and about what the word has come
to mean.)

V.D.P.: Today many speak of this organic, dynamic force in the human
spirit as unreal. They use myth as a synonym of that which is not.

P. L. T.: As synonymous with lie. I am constantly protesting against that.
What would Mantis say, I wonder, Mantis who is one of the great

embodiments of myth that you write of so often and that I remember, too, from childhood. For me she was simply a praying mantis, I did not know her as a mythical creature. But she filled me with a sense of wonder—the long narrow-waisted insect praying. I would stand for hours watching her, wondering when the prayer would end. But it never did. The saints must envy such energy! And then, when I grew up, I found Mantis in your books and knew her—or him?— for one of the Lordly Ones. Tell a little about that.

V.D.P.: Well, it's almost impossible for me to see Mantis as apart from my own beginning because of my early experience. One of the great influences in my life was a Bushman nurse, far more important to me than my own parents. I remember, as a very little boy, hearing her talking with Mantis. She was asking, in the Bushman tongue, "How high is the water?" and the mantis would put down its tiny hands.

And I protested to my nurse, "But, look, we're not near any water. We're a thousand miles from the sea. Why do you talk to Mantis about water? Does water come out of the desert?" "Well," she said, "in the beginning, water was everywhere and Mantis was nearly drowned. And a bee came and rescued him and flew and flew all day long till the sun began to go down. Then the bee looked desperately round for a place where it could put Mantis and, suddenly, there it was! A wonderful flower above the water, a flower we no longer see on this earth, and the bee put Mantis inside it. So Mantis was safe, for from there, under the power of his own wings, he could find a dry rock to sit on." . . .

(They talked about the power of healing and of the need to go on telling stories. Sir Laurens said that he knew many examples of the relationship between life and the process of story.)

P. L. T.: Tell me about the Bushman woman who came down on a cord and promised to stay with her Bushman husband as long as he did not look into her basket.

V.D.P.: One night, a man saw a group of beautiful girls coming down from the sky on a cord. Each carried a little tightly woven basket.

And one of them he caught. "Yes," she said, "I will live with you, on condition that you never look inside my basket without my permission." He agreed, but inevitably he said, "What the hell!" or the Stone Age equivalent of the phrase. And one day, when he was alone, he opened the basket, peeped inside and roared with laughter. "You have looked into the basket!" she accused him when she returned. "Yes, you silly woman, why make such a secret of it when there is nothing in it? The basket's empty." "You saw *nothing?*" She gave him a tragic look, turned her back and disappeared into the sunset. And the Bushman who told me the story said to me, "It wasn't the looking but the fact that he could not perceive in the basket all the wonders she had brought him from the stars." And that, for me, in a sense is one of the images that the story is to the human spirit. The basket brings us its star-stuff and the pundits—the intellectuals and the critics—look into it and say it's all rubbish and superstition, and that there's nothing in it.

P. L. T.: Would you accept a carpetbag coming from the stars? I had never read your story, but when Mary Poppins arrived, the children looked into her carpetbag and, like your Bushman, found it empty. And yet out of it came all her mundane daily possessions, including a camp bed! Did all that come from the stars? We do not know. Emptiness is fullness.

V.D.P.: It is, it is. And I think the use of a carpetbag is a wonderful example of what I mean by making a traditional story contemporary. That carpetbag had, in fact, a magic carpet inside it.

P. L. T.: Yes, but disguised. And from where was the magic carpet stolen? Out of the cauldron, of course! For instance, your film on the Kalahari gave me the ostrich egg, which also must have come from there. The ostrich was such a forgetful bird, you said, that she had to put one egg in front of her outside the nest to remind her of what she was doing. Later, when I was listening to the Greek Easter service on the radio, a reporter described the monks filing in, with eyes downcast, all except one, who was gazing round at the congregation. "Clearly," said the reporter, "he had forgotten the ostrich egg hanging over the altar." But how, I wondered, had the ostrich egg got there? I sensed a myth in the air. Years later, seeing a group of Coptic churches on television, all with ostrich eggs strung across the ceiling, my question arose again. I wrote to the producer, who told me that there were two schools of thought here, one that says the ostrich is a forgetful bird and another that of all the birds she is the most remembering. So, does she remember or does she forget? It almost doesn't matter. The egg, in both cases, is the reminder, and the link between my three experiences.

v.d.p.: Yes, yes, the link. However much we try to deny it, the dream goes dreaming through us. Deep in the spirit of European man there is an ostrich and it lives heraldically. Our Prince of Wales has three ostrich feathers in his crest; in Stone Age mythology, the moon was made out of the feather of an ostrich. So the ostrich, in a sense, is Prometheus, the bird from which man, Mantis and the god-hero stole the fire and brought it to man. And many primitive people in Africa believe that the sun is an egg.

P. L. T.: Is it known by whom or what it was laid?

v.d.p.: It hatches great birds! And how it was laid is not to be known. You will find this determination among instinctive people not to try to carry an act of knowing too far. They say, "This is where we must stop." And then they let the myth take over and wait till it tells them what else there is.

P. L. T.: That is what I've always found. We must stand in front of the mystery. "Take upon us," as Lear said, "the mystery of things as if we were God's spies."

v.d.p.: Yes, and if one looks at it that way, one finds the lines of communication between the storyteller of today and the first storyteller; between us and the person who dreams, or is dreamed by the universe, these lines of communication are intact. They can never, never fail.

P. L. T.: We have ancestors.

v.d.p.: We have ancestors. Long ago I sat at the feet of a Japanese storyteller and he began with "Once Upon a Time." And years later, in a night of great turmoil, the expression on his face when he said those words came back to me.

P. L. T.: The old phrase! Everywhere!

V.D.P.: And hearing it, a great peace came upon me. I was beyond space and time, everybody was a neighbor—this universal feeling of propinquity which makes the mystics speak of the forever which is now. . . ."

Excerpted from *Parabola, The Magazine of Myth and Tradition,* Vol. VII, No. 2 (Spring 1982). Reprinted by permission of the estate of P.L. Travers.

NO FORGETTING

by Jonathan Cott

THE POET Kenneth Rexroth once commented: "There are two ways of knowing, under standing and over bearing. The first is called wisdom. The second is called winning arguments." P.L. Travers follows the first way. As she herself tells us in her essay "The World of the Hero":

> To understand: for years I pondered on that word and tried to define its effect on myself. At last I came to the conclusion that what it means is the opposite of what it says; to understand is to stand under. Later I discovered that this was, in very fact, its meaning in Middle English. So, in order to understand, I come to something with my unknowing—my nakedness, if you like: I stand under it and let it teach me, rain down its truth upon me. That is, I think, what children do; they let it make room in them for a sense of justice, for the Wicked Fairy as well as the Sleeping Beauty, for dragons as well as princes.

And from the vantage point of "standing under" and "unknowing," she observes things from a source and center that lie in the country the old Scandinavian stories call East of the Sun and West of the Moon, at the moment beyond time—never and always—that the fairy tales refer to as "once upon a time."

Since fairy tales reveal us to ourselves, we return to them in order to remember and rediscover who we are. We must wake to and awaken the stories within us, much as the fairy-tale prince rouses the princess from her sleep, thereby fulfilling what P.L. Travers sees as the essential mythical requirement—"the reinstatement of the fallen world."

This, simply, has been P.L. Travers' task. And she has gone about it by allowing the truths of story and rhyme to speak for themselves and to dawn on and in us in ways we might never have expected. The author instinctively understands that what is often considered insignificant and despised may unexpectedly prove itself to be what is most valuable and revealing. (Cinderella, the Youngest Brother, the Fool.) As she has discovered: "The stories have to be loved for themselves before they will release their secrets."

In July, 1979, I visited P.L. Travers in her small house in the Chelsea section of London. Everything in her home contributes to a visitor's sensing the emptiness of plenitude and the plenitude of emptiness. This is exemplified, in her upstairs study, by several beautiful Japanese scroll and screen paintings, mostly by Sengai: a willow almost breaking in the wind; six persimmons; a cock crowing to the morning and a little hen bird nearby; the depiction of the syllable *mu* (literally meaning "not" or "without" and referring to a famous Zen koan); and the extraordinary "Ten Oxherding Pictures" (attributed to the twelfth-century Chinese Zen master Kaku-an Shi-en). This allegorical series, composed as a training guide for Chinese Buddhist monks, shows the progress of a man searching for his ox (for that which a person is or has in his or her self).

Travers took me out to her garden, where she was growing more than twenty varieties of herbs, many of which appear in *Mary Poppins in Cherry Tree Lane.* "Taste all of them," she suggested. "They will do you good." Then, as a friendly gesture, she cut off some rosemary sprigs and gave them to me: "This will last forever and bring you good luck. It means 'To Remember.'"

We conversed over tea, her voice peremptory but gentle, her words precise. She saw through my confusion, channeled my loquaciousness, and gave me some suggestions: "Accept everything that comes and make jewels of it . . . That's what I call the hero nature—you can only be the hero of your own story if you accept it totally."

• • •

JONATHAN COTT: In a biographical reminiscence, you wrote:

> My childhood, in a house overlooking sweeping fields of sugar cane, was
> full of reef's tokens—shells, palm fans, sprays of coral. My earliest mem-
> ory is of walking through the green forests of the cane, as if through a
> jungle, and of making nests—which I hoped a bird would inhabit—
> between the juicy stalks. I chewed cane, when it was ripe, as modern
> children chew gum.

P.L. TRAVERS: That's really not quite so exact. There are memories of
two different places mixed up in that passage. Alongside our house
grew a great field of weeds—members of the *Siderium* family. It had
masses of leaves on the outside, but when they fell down and dried
up, they became the material for a nest inside the stems. And I used
to nest there, thinking I was a bird. About six I was, and while I
knew I was a child, I also knew that I was a bird. And I'd sit there
brooding—it seemed like hours—my arms tightly clasped around me.
And the others would say, "She can't come, she's *laying*," just as you
might say of a blackbird, "She's brooding." Then my mother would
come and undo my limbs—this knotted little body that was busy in
its nest. "I have told you once," she would say, "and I've told you
twice—no laying at lunchtime." She never said: "No laying!" She
never said: "You're not a bird!" She never thought: "Oh, my god, she
must see a psychiatrist—my child thinks she's a wren or a kiwi!"

J.C.: This reminds me of the scene in *Friend Monkey* in which the house
is quiet and you hear the song "Greensleeves" in the distance. Then
you see Monkey, with his long arms wrapped closely around himself, feeling alone, as he remembers the forest where he was first left
alone by the other monkeys. And suddenly:

> Miss Brown-Potter at the age of ten, mumpish in her white muslin,
> stepped down from her portrait frame and came and stood beside him.
> For a long time or a short time—neither could have measured it—the
> two of them communed together, motionless as a painted child beside a
> painted monkey.

At that point, the ominous Professor McWhirter, who is trying to
steal Monkey away, tiptoes in. . . . So you have Monkey, wrapping

his arms around himself—the way *you* did when you were nesting as a child—remembering the forest, its *green* leaves.

P. L. T.: (sings) "Greensleeves was all my joy/And, oh, Greensleeves was my delight,/ Greensleeves was my heart of gold,/And who but my Lady Greensleeves?" . . . You've made the link. What I meant was that he was hearing "Greensleeves" sung by Miss Brown-Potter's parents. And you suggest that it refers to the green of the forest? Ah, think of that!

J.C.: And the nesting image of the arms around the body.

P. L. T.: Right, yes. You've hit on something so true—that the body remembers. We always think that memory is in the mind, and possibly also in the heart. But we forget that the body is the prime remembrancer. Put yourself in this gesture [puts arms around herself].

J.C.: Wilhelm Reich believed that our body contains our past, and that when you release its tension, the past, too, is released.

P. L. T.: I'm sure it's true. From my own experience. Sometimes I can find myself lying so *still* in my bed, so still, and yet so sensing the whole of my body in its quietude that I could be a plant. I could, in a way, know—though not with my mind—that my *body* knows what it's like to be a plant. I've never known what it's like to be an animal—I haven't got there yet. But I've had this extraordinary stillness quite recently in which so much inward life is flowing . . . like Dylan Thomas' "The force that through the green fuse drives the flower/Drives my green age." So still and yet so vivid. Strange that it's come to me to know this so late in life. Perhaps I knew it as a child but didn't know that I knew it. One does not, then, need to know.

J.C.: The word "truth" in ancient Greek has as one of its meanings "no forgetting."

P. L. T.: No forgetting . . . How marvelous! If I had to choose a motto, I'd choose that: No forgetting.

J.C.: It's in all your books. Monkey is remembering. And throughout the *Mary Poppins* volumes, almost everyone is remembering or forgetting to remember. "Slowly I moved at first, always sleeping and dreaming," says the newborn infant in *Mary Poppins Comes Back.* "I remembered all I had been and I thought of all I shall be. And when I had dreamed my dream I awoke and came swiftly."

P. L. T.: You've given me a real gift. You see, I get gifts every day from everywhere, and that's more precious to me than rubies. . . . But along with no forgetting, I continually sense myself as knowing less and less. To become an *un*knower would be wonderful.

J.C.: To return to your childhood and your essay "Only Connect." You write:

> In a world where there are few possessions, where nobody answers questions, where nobody explains—I say this with joy, not sorrow!—children must build life for themselves. One child is forced this way, one another. I went into imagination and poetry . . .

Now, in *Friend Monkey*, Miss Brown-Potter is described as having lived, as a child, in an attic with a nurse and then a governess—"a shy child in a white dress, isolated, plain, dreaming of far-away places." And I'm struck by the resemblance here between the passage I quoted from "Only Connect" and the childhood lives of Miss Brown-Potter and Beatrix Potter (two Potters, incidentally!).

P. L. T.: Yes, I made that connection—not in my mind but in my "no forgetting," and it came out in Miss Brown-Potter. And instinctively, with my not-knowing, I gave her the same kind of childhood as Beatrix Potter had. But she also relates to Mary Kingsley, the niece of Charles Kingsley, who went to West Africa and explored it as an anthropologist—wearing elastic-sided boots, flowing skirts, a cape, and a bonnet. She made great friends with a Scottish missionary woman, similarly dressed, and she lived contentedly amongst the tribes—in particular the Fan tribe (now called he Fang tribe). She would give the tribal women her high-necked blouses as presents, and the men wore them! When Miss Brown-Potter tells Mrs. Linnet that all she has to do to leopards is to give them a poke with her foot and they'll move on, well, I took this from Mary Kingsley. A leopard one day came sniffling around her skirts, and she said, giving it a poke with her boot, "Get along, you idiot!" and it got along at once. This to me was so marvelous. What a woman!

J.C.: There's something very lonely about the childhoods of Beatrix Potter and Miss Brown-Potter. And Louis, too—the cockatoo in *Friend Monkey*—is described as being "far from home and a stranger in the world of men." It reminds me of an extraordinary statement by Meister Eckhart:

> Pity them, my children, they are far from home and no one knows them. Let those in quest of God be careful lest appearances deceive them in these people who are peculiar and hard to place; no one rightly knows them but those in whom the same light shines.

P. L. T.: Please let me have a copy of that. Meister Eckhart is one of the greatest, greatest teachers. We're *all* far from home. Make no mistake about that. But I might as well be a clod in a forest with grass growing out of it, so at home do I feel in this world. I think it's a most beautiful world. I want no other planet, I don't want to move to a space colony. The farther I go, the more I like being here. But that doesn't prevent me from knowing full well that I'm far from home.

J.C.: "Do not fight,/But help one another/On your way—/Dear migrating birds'" wrote the Japanese poet Issa. And it seems that the little community of *Friend Monkey* is one in which each creature helps the other. Except, perhaps, the cantankerous, incorrigible, stubborn Uncle Trehunsey.

P. L. T.: I wasn't going to change or sentimentalize that uncle. He was going to live and die as himself.

J.C.: *Friend Monkey,* with all its fantastic characters, would make a wonderful film, don't you think?

P. L. T.: And I see how it could be done. They could disguise a very small man as a monkey, as they did with those animals in *Peter Rabbit and the Tales of Beatrix Potter*—a tiny man or boy in fur and a monkey face. I'd like it so much to be done as a film—but certainly not as a cartoon, for you must show the sorrow and the grief and the endless love that is in Monkey . . . it never fails. He brings disaster in his train until the very end. . . . You know, I didn't realize that Professor McWhirter wasn't a bad guy until that very end, I had no idea! It came upon me as a shock—in a garden in Virginia—and I lifted up my hands and said, "To have given me such an idea, how marvelous, where could I have got it from?" He was *not* a villain, after all, but the rescuer. Perhaps, in a sense, the villain is always the rescuer, the one who throws the story forward, like the Wicked Fairy in the Sleeping Beauty story.

J.C.: It's in this approving sense that you write about the Wise Women of fairy tales—"sisters of the Sirens, kin to the Fates and the World Mothers"—each of them an aspect of Kali, "who carries in her multiple hands the powers of good and evil." You often talk about what you call "the necessary antagonist."

P. L. T.: The necessary antagonist is always the one who brings to fruition the essential ending. What would we do without any naysayers?

J.C.: Having discovered that Professor McWhirter is not a villain, Mr. Linnet thinks to himself: "What use is the right fact when the point of view is wrong?"

P. L. T.: Yes, I'm so grateful to D.H. Lawrence. I've quoted this again and again, and think he should be canonized for saying that there's the truth of truth as well as the truth of fact. You see, everybody sees Professor McWhirter collecting and stealing the animals—that's the truth of fact—but they don't know till the end of the story that he's taking them to the secret islands in order to protect them. That's the truth of truth.

J.C.: In one tradition, the Indian monkey god Hanuman, who is the inspiration for *Friend Monkey,* is said to be the son of Shiva. And I noticed that on one of your walls you have a poster of a nineteenth-century Indian painting showing Hanuman carrying Shiva and Parvati in his heart. In this regard, there's a text I like very much which I wanted to read to you:

> For one cycle of creation Shiva dances. For the next cycle he dreams. We think we are living in the real world and Shiva is dancing. We are not. He is dreaming.

P. L. T.: It's wonderful. I must have that quotation.

J.C.: I read it to you because everywhere in the Mary Poppins books are dancers and dancing. In *Mary Poppins in the Park,* we read: "With a little push, Michael spun them round. And again, a push, and again a spin. And soon they were all revolving gently in the middle of the room." Even the world dances: "'It's love that makes the world go round!' yelled Eenie, Meenie, and Mynie. And, indeed, the world did seem to be spinning, turning for joy upon its axis, as the little Park spun round its buttercup tree. Round and round and round it went in a steady, stately movement."

P. L. T.: James Stephens said: "The first and last duty of man is to dance." And I agree with that. In my childhood, at any moment of despair or joy, I danced. And in a way I do it still . . .

J.C.: Here's a scene from *Mary Poppins Comes Back*—Mary Poppins' and the Banks children's evening out with the moon, sun, planets, and constellations:

> "Then," said Jane wonderingly, "is it true that we are here tonight or do we only think we are?"
>
> The Sun smiled again, a little sadly.
>
> "Child," he said, "seek no further! From the beginning of the world all men have asked that question. And I, who am Lord of the Sky—even I do not know the answer. I am certain only that this is the Evening Out, that the Constellations are shining in your eyes and that it is true if you think it is. . . ."
>
> "Come, dance with us, Jane and Michael!" cried the Twins. And Jane forgot her question as the four of them swung out into the ring in time with the heavenly tune.

Who, where, and what are we? Are we dreaming or dancing?

P. L. T.: Maybe both!

J.C.: Jane asked the sun a question, but where does a scene like that come from?

P. L. T.: I just put the scene down as it arrived. It comes out of something in me, but it isn't as though I invented it. Because all this is in the human bloodstream. I've talked about this many times: I think that everything that's known is in the bloodstream, which gathers itself, for three score years and ten, perhaps, into a reservoir whose physical location is about two inches below the navel, in the great bowl of the abdomen. Japanese Zen masters call it *Hara*—the original, the vital center of the man. In Celtic legend it's the Cauldron of Plenty, the Water of Life, and among the Australian aborigines it's "the dreaming."

J.C.: In the cauldron must be the Great Mother, about whom so much has been written. The poet Robert Bly says that the Great Mother is basically a union of four force fields: the Good Mother (Isis, Demeter), the Death Mother (Lilith, Hecuba), the Dancing or Ecstatic Mother (Artemis, Sophia), and the Stone or Tooth Mother (Medusa, Coatlicue). About the third type, Bly writes:

> Artemis and all the dancing mothers, all the virgin mothers, and all the visionary mothers, Diotima and Sophia, share the energy of this field. She was often called "Virgin," not because she avoided sexual joy, but [because she brought] ecstasy into the world.

and I've felt that Mary Poppins was, in this sense, a kind of Ecstatic Mother.

P. L. T.: A woman has all these things in her. And yes, it's possible, as I said in "Letter to a Learned Astrologer," to be profligate yet keep the secret sense of oneself—like Virgo. Virginity has the most wonderful power—if it is true virginity—of *intensity*, the intensity that can be seen in a person like St. Theresa of Avila. Well, I can't answer for Mary Poppins . . . perhaps she has a lover somewhere. But it doesn't matter. And it's her affair, so to speak, not mine! (Anyway, he is certainly not Bert, the Matchman, who is a supernumerary character, and there to point up aspects of Mary Poppins, not at all to aspire to her hand.)

No, people who call Mary Poppins "prudish" are wrong, I think. The word "propriety," perhaps, correctly conveys the delicacy of her character, her way of not giving things away. I was very shocked that, in the film version of *Mary Poppins*, Mrs. Banks—that featherheaded, silly little woman—is first of all shown as a suffragette! . . . but worse still is seen pulling up her skirts and displaying her underwear. It is incredible to me, in a film set in Edwardian times. And again, when Mary Poppins dances a sort of cancan on the roof with the sweeps, she swirls her skirts till all her underwear is revealed. Now, Mary

Poppins could, of course, dance a cancan, but her skirts would *certainly* know how to behave. They would obey her, don't you see?

No, she's not a repressed spinster, which is what people who call her "prudish" usually mean. Could such a one as we have been talking about be called that? A very close friend of mine, who's a poet, said to me, when we first met: "Look, let me tell you at the outset—I loathe children's books. Don't ask me to read *Mary Poppins.*" And I said to him, "Not for my sake?" "All right," he replied morosely, "send it." And after he had read it he wrote, saying: "My God, why didn't you *tell* me? Mary Poppins with her *cool, green core of sex* has me enthralled forever!"

J.C.: I know you admire the "Round Dance of Jesus" from the *Gnostic Acts of John,* a text from the early Christian movement. *The Acts* describes Jesus anticipating arrest, bringing his followers together into a circle, holding hands to dance, while he stands in the center and chants:

> I will be saved,
> And I will save. Amen.
> I will be released,
> And I will release. Amen.
> I will be wounded,
> And I will wound. Amen.
> I will be born,
> And I will bear. Amen.
> I will eat,
> And I will be eaten. Amen . . .

I quote this because I'm reminded of the speech by the Hamadryad—the serpent leader of the animals in the zoo—who tells the children in *Mary Poppins* (as they watch the animals dance the Grand Chain around Mary Poppins) that

> it may be that to eat and be eaten are the same thing in the end. My wisdom tells me that this is probably so. We are all made of the same stuff, remember, we of the Jungle, you of the City. . . . Bird and beast and stone and star—we are all one. . . . Child and serpent, star and stone—all one.

It also reminds me that in certain primitive tribes, the hunters wear the horns of the animals they are killing, identifying with them in order to create a balance between them.

P. L. T.: Wonderful. Yes.

J.C.: And in "Letter to a Learned Astrologer," writing about the sign of Aquarius, you point out that the pictorial zodiac shows us a man alone carrying "a pitcher, flagon, or amphora, the ultimate morphology of the feminine." And to hint at an explanation of the dual function of this man and his watering pot, you present the following formulation: "I will pour out." "I will be poured."

P. L. T.: Yes, I was thinking of the passage from the "Round Dance of the Cross" when I wrote that. One says, "I will be poured." That is my gesture in life—I'm happy to be poured. Happy to be a flagon that is poured out. The water of life—you baptize with it, it quenches thirst, it laves the newborn and the dead—I meant it in every way. He who pours out; and she who is poured—they're reciprocal, like Yang and Yin.

J.C.: It's a very deep passage, and I don't think I understand it fully.

P. L. T.: Nor do I. Nor do I. I wait to be told.

J.C.: Mary Poppins presents the children with certain situations; and as in initiations, the children enter into them and come out with a new understanding.

P. L. T.: Well, I feel one is taught by what one does. There's a wonderful line in a poem by Theodore Roethke which says: "You learn by going where you have to go." You can't learn before you set out, can you? You go along with the road and learn as you go. Having written certain things, I sometimes think to myself, "How did *she* learn that? It's so *true.*"

J.C.: You mean Mary Poppins?

P. L. T.: No, P. L. Travers. And I long to meet her. And then I wonder: Am I she?

J.C.: Are you?

P. L. T.: I don't know. . . .

AT HOME WITH PAMELA TRAVERS

The Radcliffe Lectures

by Philip Zaleski

THE CLOUDS loomed long and black to the north as we entered the London Underground at Paddington Station, and by the time we emerged the rain was descending in sheets. I glanced at my wife and my three-year-old son, shouted "Up umbrellas!" and we plunged into the torrent. Our destination was a pink doorway in a townhouse on a quiet, tree-lined street in Chelsea: the home of P.L. Travers.

Neither Carol, John, nor I had met Mrs. Travers, although I had corresponded with her often during my stint as an editor of *Parabola*. As we sped along the sidewalk, umbrellas inverted by the winds and hair plastered to our heads, I recalled the conflicting counsel that I had received back in the States: "She doesn't suffer fools gladly. Be sure to stay on your toes or she'll bite," warned one friend. "Nonsense!" declared another. "She's sweet as an angel, a perfect hostess." Soon I would see for myself. In the meanwhile, these reports excited me, for they assured me that, come what may, I was about to meet someone impossible to pigeonhole.

We arrived on Travers' doorstep in a sodden mass. There flashed into my mind one of the few autobiographical tidbits I knew about this very private author: her youthful pilgrimage through a drenching rainstorm to the home of William Butler Yeats, bearing as a gift a bundle of rowan branches from the Isle of Innisfree. And here were we, ready to drip in turn over Travers' fine carpets, but without any rowan to ease our passage.

Nonetheless, the door opened. We were ushered inside and soon seated in Travers' parlor. Our hostess greeted us cordially, but I felt from the first a certain distance in her demeanor—perhaps, I told myself, nothing more than Old World reserve. We talked about this and that in a desultory way, until the tea kettle began to sing on the copper. Travers started to rise and then sat down again, in obvious discomfort. "I've not been well," she said. In an instant, Carol, with that alacrity that women so often display when someone is in need, said "I'll get it" and scooted into the kitchen, where we could hear her bustling around with the tea things. Travers looked at me wryly and said, "So the host becomes the guest!"

From this moment on, our conversation soared. Travers' mind led the way, dancing from one subject to the next: mythology, children's literature, contemplative practice, the technical difficulties of writing in the first person. When Carol emerged with a tray crammed with plates, cups, and steaming pot, Travers beamed approval. She was enjoying herself at last. So this, I thought, was our rowan branch: that the guest become the host; that the ordinary become the extraordinary.

It has dawned on me since that this zest for seeing things afresh might explain the clashing descriptions of Travers that I had heard. After all, everyday magic lies at the heart of all her writing. Everywhere the unexpected reigns: in the Poppins books, where animals talk and nannies soar on the wind; in *Friend Monkey,* with the antics of its madcap protagonist; in *What the Bee Knows,* with its emphasis, at once irksome and beguiling, on what Travers calls "unknowing." What if this were Travers' method not only in the cool, impersonal medium of print but also in the more intimate milieu of lecturing, teaching, and talking? What if she tailored her conversation as she tailored her writing, to evoke the best in others? Wasn't it possible, I wondered, that Travers' use of the spoken word offered a bay window into her creative vision?

Recently, I've had the opportunity to examine some of the surviving records of her talks and interviews. Voice recordings are, alas, exceedingly rare. The few that remain reveal a soft, musical voice, enunciating with perfect diction in a British accent that contains no hint of Travers' Australian roots. She talked slowly, choosing her words with care. One senses a woman who thought before she spoke.

Happily, the dearth of recordings is balanced by a wealth of transcriptions—of talks, lectures, radio presentations, print interviews. Of special interest, and almost entirely unmined by scholars, are the minutes of the "at homes" that Travers held for American undergraduates during her stints as writer-in-residence at Radcliffe College in 1966 and as visiting writer at Smith College in 1967. These "at homes" confirm the abiding sense that Travers used every conversation as a chance to learn and—if her interlocutors were students or spiritual seekers—a chance to teach.

Even a cursory dip into the transcripts and recordings reveals important facts about Travers' conversational manner. One is that she despised small talk. Indeed, when we visited her in London, she displayed no interest in exchanging pleasantries about politics or weather. We plunged immediately into serious talk about serious things. Similarly, she disliked coyness, or anything less than honest grappling with truth. When a British radio interviewer asked her what she meant by her statement that "myths never were and always are," she shot back, "Oh, but you're just like any other interviewer. You know that [answer] yourself, perfectly well!" This is classic Travers: to employ surprise, even shock, as a teaching device. To a gathering of Radcliffe students she declared how fortunate it was that "no one had fostered her imagination." A typical bit of Travers provocation, this seems a brazen statement until one discerns her point: not that she opposed the nurturing of imagination, but that she believed this could best be accomplished by leaving the child free to discover things at its own pace. "A child needs time to learn to live in its own world," she said. "Just let it be, leave it alone to grow from its mother root."

Nor did Travers withhold tart observations that cut across cultural conventions. Speaking at Smith, a feminist stronghold, about the mixed company at her "at homes," she declared: "I like to have men come because their questions are so good, and the girls' become better when

men are present." In another "at home," she declared: "I am an anar-
chist in regard to education. . . . I think you could do just as well with
half the education you have. In a world where everybody knows everything it is comfortable to be a lunatic."

Such prickly statements are, one suspects, the source of at least some
of the negative reactions to Travers. One Smith undergraduate complained to *The New York Times:* "I haven't met her but I hear she's hard
to get along with." And an English professor grumbled, "She's as touchy
as hell. It's a mistake to say she's a beloved English writer." But what
this professor perceived as touchiness may have been, in fact, an effort
on Travers' part to elicit the best from those around her.

Imagine what it must have been like for a famous author to face a
troop of callow undergraduates in the starch-and-frill atmosphere of
Radcliffe or Smith. Yet rather than coddle her listeners, Travers took
them seriously, putting herself—or at least her likeability—on the line.
Asked by one young woman, "How did you first come to write *Mary
Poppins,*" she exclaimed, "Oh, that terrible question! It would never
occur to me to ask Carroll how he came to write about the March
Hare!" Another student asked, even more insipidly, "Where were you
born?" To this, Travers offered the wry response, "Oh, are we beginning
there? I thought perhaps somewhere in the middle; from there you can
see back to the beginning—by 'indirection find direction out,' as it
were. It's so boring to talk about facts." During the same "at home,"
she spied some students taking notes and voiced her disapproval: "People
are so used to jotting things down in notebooks—look at you two,
madly scribbling—but if it's in a notebook, it's soon forgotten."

Here one is reminded, perhaps, of young Jane's comment about her
nanny: "Mary Poppins never wasted time in being nice." Travers' aim,
as teacher and writer, was not to be nice, but to provoke, challenge,
awaken. One sees this, for example, in the "at home" record for
November 1965, in which she spoke to a small circle of Radcliffeans
about the importance of precision in language. In particular, she con-
tended that Americans should spell "center" as the English do, as
"centre," for only thus is its French ancestry revealed. To spell "center"
in the American way is to fashion a word that "has no family tree, and

I think a word ought to." For those who love the genetics of language, this is a masterful point.

But to paint the creator of Mary Poppins as a nay-sayer is to do her grave injustice. In the same set of "at homes" in which Travers skewered linguistic gaffes, she offered splendid examples of the English tongue used well by other authors. Even more to the point is her own luminous use of language. Consider this spontaneous "at home" description of an English sky: "horizons of ink and lavender and mauve and pale blue and grey very pearly and delicate . . . the light comes up out of the earth as well as down from the sky, strange and misty." Nor did Travers stint on praise, when praise is called for. Asked in a 1984 British Radio 3 interview about T.S. Eliot, she responded with a memorable paean:

> He was a wonderful man. Once I had a group of children playing football in Battersea Park. One of them said to me, "Look, look, look." And there was Eliot. One boy thought, "Oh I can get an autograph." I remember so well Eliot, with a stump of a pencil that was handed to him, writing his name ceremoniously and most beautifully—bending over graciously, as God might bend over—on a piece of paper balanced on a football. It was a wonderful picture, so graceful, so benign.

Travers, too, could be benign, even at the expense of her privacy. Consider the note tacked to the bulletin board of the residential house in which she lived while at Smith College: "A happy Thanksgiving to you all. I am always at home to anyone in Lamont who would like to come at any time. Just knock on my door and welcome."

Such instances could be multiplied. But the point isn't to ascertain whether Travers was charming or harsh. The point isn't her personality at all, but rather her extraordinary methods for working with others. To bring out the best in herself and her interlocutors, she would cajole, entice, dazzle. Here her ability to leap from one subject to another— touching each just long enough to awaken her listeners' interest.

For example, she began one session with Radcliffe undergraduates by describing a marionette play she had in mind to write, based on the parable of the Prodigal Son. During her description she offered, in an off-hand way, a radical new interpretation of the son who stays at home

172

as "the central part of a man," the part "that never needed to go out." Then, while the students digested this insight, Travers switched gears entirely, admiring the stockings on one of her young listeners and declaring, "I would like to take some of those back to England, to a girl who would look marvelous in them." As the students' minds shifted towards legwear, Travers leap-frogged back to the Prodigal Son and its meaning for us today, ensuring that her listeners remained alert, attentive to the changing patterns of thought.

Paradox was another tool that Travers favored. In her case, we might define paradox as a refusal to say "yes" or "no" when neither will suffice; as a mature surrender to the mysterious workings of the world. As she wrote in "Letter to a Learned Astrologer," "I had to learn that to be . . . defenseless is the only way to safety; that the sieve knows a lot about water, emptiness of plenitude. . . ." Paradox ruled her literary world, epitomized by the prim, plain nanny who flies at will and converses with animals. It ran in pronounced fashion through her conversations as well: "Growing up, it seems to me, is in a way growing-down. You begin by being clever, knowing it all and gradually you come to realize that you know nothing."

In the same vein, Travers preferred questions to answers. She once declared, "Anything I write is all question. I don't think I have the answers." And on a British radio program she told her interviewer, "I feel myself to be an unknower. I don't know things with my head." She says goodbye, at the conclusion of her final Radcliffe "at home," with the gift of an enigma: "Life is the writer's education. . . . That and knowing the alphabet. 'All that is or was or will be lies between A and Z.' Where does that come from?"

And so it was for us in her London home. After chatting with the grown-ups, Travers turned her attention to little John, who had been fidgeting throughout our conversation. She escorted him around the room, showing him wall-hangings and scattered toys, and then invited him to mount her small wooden rocking horse. "This horse," she said, "is named Mervyn." John looked quizzically at her and clambered on. We saw his uncertainty as the horse's center of gravity shifted under his weight. Travers looked him in the eyes ("very few people look you in the eyes. Have you noticed? It takes courage!" she observed in one interview), and asked, "How can you keep your balance? That's the question, how to find your balance?" John considered this for a moment. Then he grinned, and rocked in sheer delight.

PART SIX

THREE ARTICLES BY
P.L. TRAVERS

I NEVER WROTE FOR CHILDREN

NOT LONG AGO, an American journalist who is writing a book on children's books asked me for my "general ideas on literature for children, my aims and purposes and what led me to the field." Well, this flummoxed me. I hadn't any ideas, general or specific, on literature for children and I did not set out with aims or purposes. I couldn't say that anything I had done was intended or invented. It has simply happened. Furthermore, I told him that I was not at all sure that I was in his field, even though children throughout the world have, some of them, been kind enough to read what I write. I said that it was a strong belief of mine that I didn't write for children at all, that the idea simply didn't enter my head. I am bound to assume, of course, that there is such a field—I hear about it so often—but I wonder if it is a valid one or whether it has not been created less by writers than by publishers and booksellers. I am always astonished when I see books labeled for "From 5 to 7" or "From 9 to 12," because who is to know what child will be moved by what book and at what age? Who is to be the judge?

Nothing I had written before *Mary Poppins* had anything to do with children, and I have always assumed, when I thought about it at all, that she had come out of the same well of nothingness as the poetry, myth, and legend that had absorbed me all my writing life. If I had been told while I was working on the book that I was doing it for children, I think I would have been terrified. How would I have had the effrontery to attempt such a thing? For, if for children, the question inevitably arises: "For what children?" That word "children" is a large blanket; it covers, as with the word "grown-ups," every kind of being that exists. Was I writing for Japanese children, telling a race of people who have no staircases in their houses about somebody who slid up the banisters? For the children in Africa who read it in Swahili and who have never even seen an umbrella, much less used one? Or to come to those nearer my own world, was I writing for the boy who wrote to me with such noble anger when he came to the end of the third book—"Madam, you have sent Mary Poppins away. Madam, I will never forgive you. You have made the children cry." What a reproach, what a picture—the children weeping in the world, and I responsible. Could I ever have intended to write for such a child?

A writer is, after all, only half his book. The other half is the reader, and from the reader the writer learns. I remember a boy of sixteen who knew me well asking me earnestly to make him a promise. Hesitantly, I promised, uncertain as to where it would lead me. Then he said, "Promise me never to be clever. I have just read *Mary Poppins* again and I have come to the conclusion that it could only have been written by a lunatic." I accepted this, as I believe he meant it, as high praise. And again a reader had given me a clue. Moonstruck! One has to be moonstruck, which is to say, absorbed in, lost in, and in love with one's own material. Perhaps that is how it is done.

If I go back to my own childhood—no, not back, but if I, as it were, turn sideways and consult it (James Joyce once wrote, "My childhood bends beside me")—I am once again confronted with the question of who writes for children. We had very few books in our family nursery. All the Beatrix Potters, the Nesbits, and the two Alices, all of which I loved then and still love, for there is nothing in them that I have left behind or rejected as belonging specifically to childhood. Of course, there were the fairy tales, and on my father's shelves there were rows of Dickens and Scott which I inched my way through simply because they were something to read. There was also, now I come to think of it, Heinrich Hoffmann's "Struwwelpeter," which is now thought to be cruel. But nothing in him frightened me. My parents, I knew, would never let me be drowned in ink or have my thumb cut off by the Great Long Red-Legged Scissor Man. It is worth asking, I think, why we grown-ups have become so timid that we bowdlerize, blot out, retell, and gut the real stories for fear that truth, with its terrible beauty, should burst upon the children. Perhaps it is because we have lived through a period of such horror and violence that we tremble at the thought of inflicting truth upon the young. But children have strong stomachs. They need to know what is true.

I had a strong stomach myself, for as well as the unbowdlerized fairy tales, I had a great affection for a book I found on my father's shelf called "Twelve Deathbed Scenes." I read it so often that I knew it by heart, each death being more lugubrious and more edifying than the one before it. I used to long to die, on condition, of course, that I came alive again the next minute, to see if I, too, could pass away with equal misery and grandeur. I wonder about the author of that book. Nobody in his lifetime could possibly have told him that he was a writer for children. He would not have made such a claim himself. Yet, in a sense, he was writing for children since one loving reader ten years of age was keeping his memory green.

It was the same with my mother's novels. Every afternoon, when she took her siesta, I would slip into her room, avidly read for half an hour and sneak away just as she was waking. Those books fascinated me, not because they were so interesting but because they were so dull. They dealt exclusively with one subject, which seemed to be a kind of loving. But love to me was what the sea is to a fish; something you swim in while you are going about the important affairs of life. The characters were all stationary figures; like waxworks, they never did anything, never went anywhere, never played games as far as I could see, no teeth were ever brushed, no one was reminded to wash his hands, and if they ever went to bed it was not explicitly stated; or else they went to bed willingly but surreptitiously, often with dire unspecified results and amid general disapprobation. I looked forward to those stolen half-hours as, I suppose, a drunkard does to a drinking bout—not so much with pleasure as a kind of enthrallment. I was ensnared, as a snake is by a snakecharmer, by such a distorted view of life. But what of the

179

authors? Did they, as they poured out their hearts with so much zest, see themselves as writers for children? Surely not. Yet for one child—indeed they were.

And what about the Bible, that black leatherbound book that was left about presumably on the supposition that no child being provided, as I was, with brightly colored retellings from it would want to read the original. But the black book fascinated me, perhaps because there was an air about it as of something forbidden. I spurned the gutted children's version and went looking for enormous terrible facts. Tellings, anyway, are always diminishments. They present the lively plot of the story but omit the curious splendors—beheaded drunk in the pavilions; Jezebel eaten by dogs at the wall; the Beast that was, is not, yet is; harlots, unicorns. Don't think that I understood it—how could I? But the Bible's trumpets breached my inner walls and the potent brew came swirling in to mix with fairy tales and myths and whatever stuff was in me.

Of course, if you let a child read the Bible it will inevitably put the grown-ups in precarious positions.

"What," I asked my father once, "what is a concubine?"

"Er-hum—!" he responded. "Why do you ask?" Clearly, he was playing for time.

"Well, it says in the Bible that David took him more concubines and Solomon had three hundred."

He inwardly groaned, but grappled with it. "Well, David was the head of the house, he needed people to look after him and the concubines—er—did."

Three hundred! I thought to myself. One would need a very big house.

"What a pity, father, that you have only two!"

He was astonished. "Two what?"

"Two concubines—Katie and Bella to cook and make beds."

"Katie and Bella are *not* my concubines." Here was a child being childish, which was something he did not like.

"Then, Nelly, what about her?" Nelly was slightly wanting, and came to help with the washing.

"Certainly not." The idea was repugnant.

"Well, father, who *are* your concubines?"

"I *have* no concubines!" he roared and stormed out of the room.

The head of the house and no concubines! Clearly we, as a family, were vastly lower on the social scale than Solomon or David.

And so I was left to deal with the mighty questions myself. Hath the rain a father, who hath begotten the drops of dew; where wert thou when I laid the foundations of the earth? I had to be a good deal older before I understood that the questions were, in the largest sense, rhetorical. No, the Bible was not written for children, but a stray child, here and there, will take it for its own.

Who, then, does write for children? One can, of course, point to the dedication pages as proof positive that somebody does. One thinks of Beatrix Potter's Noel, and Hugh Lofting's children. But I wonder if such names are not really a sort of smokescreen. A dedication, after all, is not a starting point but rather a last grand flourish. You do not write a book for this or that person, you offer it to him afterward. Nothing will persuade me, in spite of all his poetic protestations, that Lewis Carroll wrote his books for Alice, or, indeed, for any child. Alice was the occasion but not the cause of his long, involved, many-leveled confabulations with the curious inner world of Charles Lutwidge Dodgson. Of course, when it was all over, when he had safely committed it to paper, he could afford a benignant smile and the assurance that it had been done for children. But do you really believe that?

It is also possible that these dedicatory names may be a form of unconscious appeasement, perhaps even of self-protection. A writer can excuse himself to society for having invented the push me-pull you, an animal with a head at both ends, by saying with an offhand laugh, "After all, it's for children." And if a man happens to find himself in the company of a white rabbit, elegantly waistcoated and wearing a watch, scurrying down a dark tunnel and afraid of being late for the party, he does well to slap a child's name on the book. He may thus hope to get off lightly.

But in the long run truth will out, as it did when Beatrix Potter declared, "I write to please myself!"—a statement as grand and absolute, in its own way, as Galileo's legendary "It moves, nevertheless." There is, if you notice, a special flavor, a smack of inner self-delight, about the things people write to please themselves—think of Milne, think of Tolkien, think of Laura Ingalls Wilder—those books not written for children that children purloin and make their own.

For a long time I thought that this declaration—"I write to please myself," backed up by C.S. Lewis' statement that a book that is written solely for children is by definition a bad book—were the last words on the subject. But the more I brooded the more I saw that, as far as I was concerned, neither of these comments was the complete answer. And then, by chance, I turned on the television one evening and found Maurice Sendak being interviewed about his book *Where the Wild Things Are*. All the usual irrelevant questions were being flung at him— do you like children, have you children of your own? And to my astonishment I heard my own voice calling to him in the empty room. "You have been a child. Tell them that!" And his screen image, after a short pause, said simply and with dignity, "I have been a child." It was magical. He couldn't possibly have heard me and yet—distant in space but at the same moment of time, we had both come to the same point. "I have been a child."

Now, I don't at all mean by this that the people who write—how should I put it?—the books that children read are doing it for the child they were. Nothing so nostalgic, nothing so self-indulgent, nothing so sentimental. But isn't there, here, a kind of clue? To be aware of having been a child—and who am I but the child I was, wounded, scarred and dirtied over, but still essentially that child, for essence cannot change—to be aware of and in touch with this fact is to have the whole long body of one's life at one's disposal, complete and unfragmented. You do not chop off a section of your imaginative substance and make a book specifically for children for—if you are honest—you have, in fact, no idea where childhood ends and maturity begins. It is all endless and all one. And from time to time, without intention or invention, this whole body of stuff, each part constantly cross-fertilizing every other, sends up—what is the right word?—intimations. And the best you can do, if you are lucky, is to be there to jot them down. This being there, this being present, is important, otherwise they are lost.

Your role is that of the necessary lunatic who remains attentive and in readiness, unself-conscious, unconcerned, all disbelief suspended, even when frogs turn into princes and when nursemaids, against all gravity, slide up the banisters. Indeed, on a certain level (not immediately accessible, perhaps, but one which we deride at our peril), the frog is lawfully a prince and the transcending of the laws of gravity—up the banisters or up the glass mountain, it really makes no difference—is the proper task of the hero. And heroes and their concomitant villains are the stuff of literature.

These matters, I submit, have nothing to do with the label "From 5 to 7"; they have nothing to do with age at all, unless they refer to all ages. Nor have they anything to do with that other label, "Literature for Children," which suggests that this is something different from literature in general, something that pens off both child and author from the mainstream of writing. This seems to me hard both on children and on literature. For if it is literature at all, it can't help being all one river and you put into it, according to age, a small foot or a large one. When mine was a small foot, I seem to remember that I was grateful for books that did not speak to my childishness, books that treated me with respect, that spread out the story just as it was—Grimm's Fairy Tales, for instance—and left me to deal with the matter as well as I could. If they moralized, I was not offended. I let them do it because of the story and promptly forgot the moral. If they tried to explain, I humored them, again for the sake of the story. Book and reader communed together, each accepting the other. So, remembering my own experience as a reader, could I, as a writer, speak to a child by way of his childishness?

Childlikeness—ah, that is another matter. It is a quality that can be found in child and grown-up alike. It has nothing to do with age. Not very long ago, a woman journalist came to see me and told me how she had read *Mary Poppins* to her child very quietly so as not to disturb the father who was working in the same room. And night after night, with increasing irascibility, the father protested against this surreptitiousness. He was not being disturbed, he said, and begged her not to mumble. If there was one thing he detested, he said, it was the sound of somebody mumbling. And after a week of such protestations, when he was going away for a night, he took the child aside and whispered, "Listen carefully to the story and when I come back you can tell me all that has happened." He, himself, had been listening all the time.

I have a feeling of affection for that father, for I think there was something in him that would agree with me, if I put it to him, that what is real is real for everyone, not only but *also* for children. And he would not, I think, call me frivolous if I suggested that the country mentioned in "Rumpelstiltskin," where the fox and the hare say good night to each other—that this country is the place we are all seeking, child and grown-up alike. Perhaps we are looking for miracles. Most certainly we are looking for meaning. We want the fox not to eat the hare, we want the opposites reconciled. Child and grown-up alike, we want it. And I hope *you* will not think me frivolous when I say that it is not only children but many grown-ups—lunatic grown-ups, if you will—who in their own inner worlds are concerned at the Sleeping Beauty's sleep and long for her to be wakened.

And here it is worthwhile remembering, since we are on the subject of Not Writing for Children, that neither "The Sleeping Beauty" nor "Rumpelstiltskin" was originally written for children. In fact, none of the fundamental fairy stories were ever written at all. They arose spontaneously from the folk and were transmitted orally from generation to generation to unlettered listeners of all ages. It was not until the nineteenth century, when the collectors set them down in print, that the children purloined them and made them their own. They were the perquisites of the grown-ups, and the children simply took them. I remember a poem of Walter de la Mare's that begins, "I'll sing you a song of the world's little children magic has stolen away." Well, I could sing you a song of the world's magic children have stolen away. For in the long run it is children themselves who decide what they want. They put out their hands and abstract the treasure from all sorts of likely and unlikely places, as I have tried to show.

So, confronted with this hoard of stolen riches, the question of who writes or who does not write for children becomes unimportant and, in fact, irrelevant. For every book is a message, and if children happen

184

to receive and like it, they will appropriate it to themselves no matter what the author may say or what label he gives himself. And those who, against all odds—and I'm one of them—protest that they do not write for children, cannot help being aware of this fact and are, I assure you, grateful.

Originally published in *The New York Times Magazine,* July 2, 1978
Reprinted by permission of the Estate of P.L. Travers

MYTH, SYMBOL, AND TRADITION

IN SPEAKING of the traditions, I speak not as an anthropologist or a doctor of divinity or a historian of comparative religion—nothing as grand as any of these—but simply as a storyteller. My way of approaching the traditions is a storyteller's way—through the myth, legend, folklore, and indeed the fairy tale to which they are so inextricably bound.

Anything I have to say, therefore, will come from the same storehouse as those chronicles we refer to, always pejoratively, I'm afraid, as Old Wives' Tales and Superstition.

But can we, I wonder, dismiss these lightly? What, after all, is superstition? If we examine it, at its root we will find that the word comes from *super stitia*—that which stands over; therefore, by extension, that which remains, the last tail-end of something that has in the past had truth and meaning; a part that has by chance escaped the holocaust of time and which, since it is only a part, is inevitably misunderstood and very often reviled as meaningless. But may there not be a positive side to superstition? Perhaps if we could grasp that tail and patiently let it draw us backward, we might come upon the main body, its very head and source.

As to Old Wives, we do wrong to ignore our debt to them. I speak feelingly because, being a storyteller, I am inevitably something of an Old Wife myself! And who else, other than Old Wives, has preserved for us all the myth and folklore, all the fairy tales, and all the legends that are wound about the great traditions as thread is wound round a spindle; those records that, far from being out of date and unscientific, are the true facts of that inner world, unseen but nearer than a man's neck vein, that interpenetrates our lives at every level and fructifies our dreams.

You will realize, of course, that here I am speaking figuratively, that Old Wives in this connection are not just a bunch of gray-haired grandmothers spinning stories in rocking chairs, but all the chroniclers from the beginning of time—named or unnamed, it doesn't matter—who have handed down by word or pen the annals of man's inner life. You will find their footprints everywhere, even—or perhaps I should say particularly—in the minuscule world of childhood, where even the games and nursery rhymes come straight out of myth and tradition.

Take as an example the old song "London Bridge Is Falling Down." This singing game, often known nowadays as "Oranges and Lemons," was played and sung under one name or another before London even existed. Sometimes it was known as "Angels and Devils"; in France it is still called "Heaven and Hell" and in Germany "Sun and Moon," but always it concerns a bridge. For our ancient forefathers, as the Old Wives tell us, attached great importance—a spiritual importance—to bridges. The Devil, it seems—or to put it more mythologically, the elemental spirit of the land who detests any interference with the natural world and prefers to divide rather than to connect—had a strong aversion to bridges. His repeated efforts to bring them to ruin called for substantial placatory offerings, even at times human sacrifice. For it was widely believed that the soul, when separated from the body, had to cross a bridge on its perilous journey from one world to the next. At all costs, therefore, London Bridge—build it up with stone so strong!—and all other bridges had to be kept in existence lest the soul should fall into enemy hands on its way toward the angel. So you see how even a children's game can lead us back, by its single thread, into a world of meaning.

And what of that old nursery riddle, "How Many Miles to Babylon?" Why Babylon, one has to ask, a city dead for thousands of years, and why should we want to go there? But when one remembers that the word Babylon means "the gate of God," the following line, "Three score and ten"—the biblical span of a man's life—seems the only possible answer. A lifetime to get to Babylon! Three score years and ten to get to the gate of God. You see what the riddle is telling us. You see how Mother Goose lifts her wings and carries us back to antiquity!

These and their like are indeed tail-ends, but tail-ends that are the residue of a vast and potent body of teaching that once so pervaded every aspect of life that the smallest child was aware of it.

Does, this, then, mean that we have to become as little children in order to discover it afresh? I think it does, in the sense that we have to find again in ourselves the child that asked, "Why was I born?" and "What is my meaning?" The questions, of course, are still there, though silted over by all the triviality of life, all the desacralization. But, para-doxically, that desacralization can, if we examine it, point us a path to the sacred—just as the negative declaration that God is dead is, in fact, a positive assurance that God has at some time been alive. The oppo-sites invoke each other. And "Danger itself," as Hölderlin said, "calls forth the rescuing power." Or, as Mircea Eliade has so rightly put it, "The man who has made his choice in favor of a profane life never succeeds entirely in doing away with religious behavior. Even the most desacralized existence still preserves traces of a religious valorization of the world"; and, further, that "myth and symbol are the very stuff of spiritual life. They may be disguised, mutilated, and depraved but are never extirpated."

It is true. The myths and traditions are in our blood, deny them though we will. After all, though we have largely forgotten that the very word means "Christ's mass," we still celebrate Christmas. The giv-ing of gifts, whether or not we care to remember it, commemorates the gifts of the Wise Men, of gold, frankincense, and myrrh. But our feasting and the decking of a green tree have an even older root. They recall to us our archaic fathers, whose Saturnalia at the winter solstice, the darkest of all times of the year, was a ritual calling back of the sun as a preparation for spring.

As for kissing under the mistletoe at this season, it hearkens right back to the time of the Druids for whom the mistletoe was a sacred plant, a plant homologized to the sun. The golden bough, by means of which Aeneas was able to pass through the underworld and return alive to the light of day, was a branch of mistletoe. And it was a sprig of mistletoe, the one plant that had not promised not to harm him, that killed Baldur the Beautiful, the god of light of the Northern myths. It is for all these reasons—to partake of the ancient Druid magic, to pass from darkness into light, and to keep each other from being harmed— that we make the placatory gesture.

It is the same with our New Year festivities. All the noise and clamor, the farewells and the greeting, all the making of good resolutions are a reminder of the myth of eternal return, the periodic destruction and recreation of the cosmos, common not only to primitive but to all religions, when the world and time and man himself, after a ritual pause, were ritually renewed.

I only began to think about this ritual pause after I had in fact written a story embodying it. As a mere storyteller perhaps I may be permitted to tell a mere story. There is in one of my books a New Year chapter called "Happy Ever After." A child asks, "When does the old year end?" "On the first stroke of midnight," says Mary Poppins. "And the new year—when does it begin?" "On the last stroke of midnight," says Mary Poppins. "Well, what then happens in between while the clock is striking twelve?" Well, what did happen in between? In asking the conundrum the child and, of course, the storyteller had happened upon the ritual pause. In the story the pause is called the Crack. And the Crack is in effect synonymous with the country spoken of in "Rumpelstiltskin," "where the fox and the hare say good night to each other"—in a word, the country where the opposites are reconciled. Red Riding Hood and the Wolf are friends, the lion and the unicorn cease fighting for the crown, the Sleeping Beauty and the Wicked Fairy lean over and kiss each other. And the Farmer's Wife, for a few brief strokes of the clock, puts away her carving knife and spares the Three Blind Mice. The Crack is, in fact, the place and the time; perhaps—I thought—the only place and the only time when to be Happy Ever After is possible and true.

Long after I had written this chapter about the ritual pause I listened to a roving reporter on the radio telling of how he had visited an African tribe at the end of *their* solar year. He described the chanting and the drumming and how at a given moment all this suddenly ceased while the gods invisibly withdrew. For a few moments there was complete silence. Then the drums broke out again in triumph, acclaiming the gods as they returned to rule over another year. "And," added the reporter, "though I do not ask you to believe it, I can vouch for the fact that my tape-recorder, for those few moments of ritual silence, ceased spinning and was still!" Well, as one who has a sort of sneaking respect for superstition, I found that I could believe it. Just as there is in Yoga practice the ritual pause in the held breath between the breathing out and the breathing in. Between one lifetime and the next, between one breath-time and the next, something waits for a moment.

Our profane life is full of these hidden meanings, of clues that we constantly overlook because we do not know what to look for. Brides are still lifted over thresholds for fear that they should stumble. But who knows why? Who remembers that thresholds, whether in human habitations or in temples and churches, were in old times places of significance? The threshold is the frontier between two worlds where sacred and profane at the same moment oppose and communicate with each other, where one world begins and another ends. To stumble at such a meeting-place would surely by unpropitious; one *needs* to be lifted over.

And marriage itself, while occasionally still a sacrament in what remains of our Christian world, is also a pattern or paradigm of something very much older—the mythical mating of the sky god and the earth goddess and the interaction of Yang and Yin, the male and female principles, from whose meeting, in the words of the *Tao Te-Ching,* come all the ten thousand things. Which means to say everything that exists.

Even house warmings, wholly secular though they now are, hold a faint memory of the poured libations by means of which religious man, in making a place for himself to dwell in—and thereby imitating the act of world-creation—invoked the blessing of the gods.

And what of the mythical structures that underlie the mass media, especially in the United States? Every comic strip presents a modern version of the mythological hero. One has only to think of the popularity of Superman or Batman or Dick Tracy to realize that, far from being dead, myth—though in a degraded form—is still vigorous and alive and actively willed and wished for.

It is the same with the novel and the detective story. The need for the hero and heroine in one and the hero and villain in the other is the age-old need, camouflaged and profane as it is, for mythological worlds and times.

Even the modern reverence for—one might almost say worship of—sport has in it a taste, a flavor, or at any rate the ghost of a flavor, of the Greek and Roman games, the principal purpose of which was to maintain a sacred energy with which the life of Nature, or of a human group or an important personage was connected. The games were a ritual, either in salute to the illustrious living or in memory of the illustrious dead, by means of which the world of the gods as well as the worlds of the dead and the living were periodically rejuvenated.

One could go on and on with examples—all the primal stuff that we have forgotten, all the meaning that has been let fall into the subterranean layers of the mind. In order to fish it up we have to become once more aware, as our ancient fathers were well aware, that by the mere fact of having a body, the mere fact of being born, each of us has assumed a place in the universe and is part of all that is. The myths and their attendant symbols can help us to find and understand this place.

It should be recognized here that myth is not used in its contemporary sense of "fiction" or "illusion" but myth as it was originally understood, myth as primordial reality, myth as revelation and precedent, myth as a model to be imitated.

"It is not," as Nietzsche said, "that there is some hidden thought or idea at the bottom of myth, as some people have supposed, but the myth itself is a kind or style of thinking. It imports an idea of the universe in its sequence of events, actions, and sufferings."

That phrase "a kind of thinking" is wonderfully apt, for it is a fact that there are things and events that cannot be described other than mythologically. Not long ago I watched a scientist on television turning himself almost inside out in his effort to find the right words to describe the birth and the death of the universe. At last he said reluctantly, as though ashamed of the unscientific statement, "It is as though it was breathed out and then breathed in again." He did not go so far as to say by whom the breathing was done: it was clear that he had never heard of the myth of the days and nights of Brahma. It arose and spoke itself in him. Science, in its efforts to explain the inexplicable, is always in danger of explaining it away. It has never heard of the Chinese ideogram Pai, which in one context means "explain" and in another "in vain." In vain to explain, how marvelous!

One could also say of myth that as well as showing man his place in the universe, it is designed to make him aware of the fact that he is meant to be something more than his own personal history and, more especially, to place him squarely between the two opposing forces that keep him and the world in balance. For this cosmic dialectic between good and evil, hero and villain, is a major theme of all mythology—the two Earth Shapers, one bounteous, all-giving, and healing; the other producing the diseases and troubles of every kind and order— the benign and the malignant interacting, balancing and checking and disciplining each other to produce a viable world. One has only to think of the Greek myth of Prometheus—forethought—and his brother Epimetheus—afterthought; of Ahura Mazda and the Zoroastrians of Persia, who stands for the power of good over against Angra Mainyu, the power of evil; of Vishnu the preserver and Shiva the destroyer as one finds them in Hindu myth; of the angels and devils of Christianity or of the two heroes of the Navaho Indian myth—Water-Child, the son of the rivers, and Monster-Slayer, born of fire—the life-giving sap of one tempering the solar aspect of the other. And all these pairs, and countless others, can be subsumed under the Chinese symbol of the Great Ultimate, which Zen has purloined and made its own, the white fish with black eye, black fish with white eye within the encompassing and reconciling circle.

Myths come, it is true, from the ancient past, but it is no less true that they, like the traditions round which they gather, are constantly being rediscovered, renewed, and restated.

One has only to think of the movement for Women's Liberation, whose groundswell is being felt throughout the world, to understand myth in action, myth working in a contemporary setting. Consider. The Great Goddess, mother and origin of all deities, the first to arise and the first to be worshipped, has long been subjugated by the masculine gods—too long, apparently, for her. Now she has had enough of it, she has flung their feet from off her neck and is rising in her wrath. A myth denied is taking its revenge and is now in the process of being resuscitated and relived.

She has waited long, the divine mother. But the myths can afford to bide their time, for ultimately they are timeless. So also, in spite of all that has accrued to them from history, are the traditions. It is impossible to speak of either as having been invented but rather that, in the words of a Zen *koan,* they were not created but summoned.

Carl Gustav Jung has written, "One could almost say that if all the world's traditions were cut off at a single blow, the whole mythology and the whole history of religion would start all over again with the next generation."

What a wonderful statement to have almost made! The traditions, like the myths, exist whether you and I note them or forget them, as the River Ganges is always flowing whether we bathe in it or not. We need no new traditions, only to understand the purport of those we have. And even if the traditions were lost, the very children would refashion them. A young man whom I know well began a story when he was about five with "It happened in the first world." And when I asked tentatively, dreading to break the thread between his words and his inner kingdom, "Tell me, is there a second?" he answered with the utmost assurance and a look of astonishment at my apparent ignorance, "Yes, of course, there are three of them. That one, this, and another." But no one had spoken to him of the three worlds, no one had spoken of the soul; no one had told him that man comes to this world from afar and still has far to go. He knew it without the telling.

It was this same child who invited, or rather required me, to play a part in a drama that he and his friends were enacting. "What is the name of the play?" I asked and was told that it was the story of Finn

MacCool. Finn MacCool is one of the great chieftains of Irish legend. "And we need you," he said, "for the Virgin Mary, the mother of Finn MacCool."

My surprise at such a juxtaposition of characters was only momentary, for I realized that in a world where everything is myth it had a kind of logic. Since the Virgin Mary had given birth to one great hero of the world why not, in the child's mind, to an endless race of heroes? D.H. Lawrence, I remembered, had made a distinction between the truth of fact and the truth of truth. The truth of fact is history; it records the dates of kings and battles; but the truth of truth has the whole of mythology for its realm. The child, in this world, was within his rights.

That same truth of truth was at work in a short essay that was recently sent me by a schoolteacher from the pen of one of her younger pupils. "The Lord," it said, "is the father of all things and Mary Poppins is the mother of all things and they are married—or has [*sic*] been married—and they are both a miracle." Well, we, of course, can laugh at this but the pupil was busy with his own mythology, adjusting it to his inner perception and arranging for his own satisfaction that his two favorite characters should together create the world.

I remember, too, the daughter of some friends of mine who, being convinced atheists, had carefully protected their offspring from any virus of religion. One day the child was discovered carefully and cautiously hiding something under a corner of the carpet, and her parents were horrified to find that the object was a small cross made of two sticks tied with string. "But why?" they demanded, in outraged voices. "I love it!" she answered simply, as she slipped the treasure under her pillow for safety. By some means that Jung, perhaps, would have understood when he said that "one must be able to let things happen in the psyche," she had found her way to one of the most ancient of all symbols—far older than Christianity. As children, we know more than we know we know. But even when we have lost what we know—or repressed it into the depths of our being—it is possible for any strong and deep experience to awaken the myths and symbols and align us to a tradition—this one or that, it hardly matters; our psychic need will choose.

For tradition itself is a unitary whole and its separate aspects are, as it were, dialects of one and the same language of the spirit. This is borne out by the similarity, the brotherly likeness that is to be found between the symbols of all traditions. Take, for instance, the Omphalos, the navel of the earth. Every holy place in every tradition is looked upon as a center of the world, a place were the sacred enters the profane, where the immeasurable is reflected back to that which can be measured and the energy of eternity pours itself into time—Mount Olympus, for instance, from which the Greek gods descended to the earth; Mount Meru of the Hindus, Mount Zion and Mount Tabor in Palestine; the Rock of Jerusalem, which was thought to be the navel from which the whole earth originally unfolded; the Field of Golgotha, which is homologized to the Garden of Eden in order that the new Adam could be crucified at the place where the old Adam was created; the Kaaba in Mecca, the sacred spot of the world community of Islam; Borobodur, the great Buddhist navel in Java; the sacred lodge of the Algonquin Indians; the underground kiva of the Hopis. One could go on with this list forever for, as Mircea Eliade has truly said, "The multiplicity or even infinity of centers of the world raises no difficulty for religious thought, concerned as it is not with geometrical or geographical space but with existential and sacred space." Therefore it can be said that for religious man his temple, his cathedral, his church, his dwelling house, even, indeed, his own body is symbolically situated at the center of the world. For where is the spring, where are the hearth and home of myth, tradition, and symbol? Where else could these be but in man himself? How could they be outside him?

Another symbol common to all traditions and one to which the navel spot can be assimilated is the cosmic axis—that axis which, in whatever form it takes, connects the three worlds—the underworld, earth, and Heaven. Sometimes, as in Dante, it is a mountain whose roots are in the Inferno and whose head is in Paradise. In many traditions it takes the form of a cosmic pillar. One thinks of the famous pillar that the Saxons called Irminsul and which was held by them to support all things and that Charlemagne so irreligiously destroyed; the *skambha,* the cosmic pillar of the Rig Veda, the earliest of the Hindu scriptures; the great Roman pillars, and the obelisks of Egypt. And there are certain Australian tribes that carry with them on their wanderings a sacred pole that supports their world and ensures continuous communication with the world of the sky. The spires of Gothic cathedrals and the minarets of Islamic mosques serve the same purpose, so do the ziggurats of Persia. They are all cosmic pillars. Even the Milky Way was in ancient times held to be a path or pillar. And in old British maps, one can find Watling Street, which is still one of the thoroughfares of the city of London, continuing all the way through Europe and ending up in the Milky Way. How graphically the point is made here that there is no discontinuity between one world and another, no break in the path of pilgrim man on his way from earth to Heaven. The pillar-path is everywhere. Among the North American Indians and the Mongolians of Northern Asia it is symbolized by the central post of the human habitation; for the herdsmen of Central Asia the path of the smoke through an opening at the top of the tent—or yurt—serves the same purpose. And one cannot go far in Mexico without coming upon wooden posts set up and notched with many steps by which the shaman, serving as man's intermediary between what is lower and what is higher, can take off on his magical climb from one world to another.

A variant of the cosmic pillar and one that serves the same purpose is the continually recurring symbol of the World Tree. In the ancient Norse and Teutonic myths the universe is supported by the great tree Yggdrasil, which extends from the nether world to the very top of Heaven. One of its roots is grounded in the fountain of Mimir, from whose sacred waters flows all the wisdom of the world. Close to another root dwell the Norns—who are the equivalent of the Greek Fates. And at the foot of the third lies the lake of memory and premonition, to achieve which qualities the high god Odin paid the price of one of his eyes. In one of the oldest Norse sagas it is said that "King Volsung let build a noble hall in such wise that a big oak tree stood therein and that the limbs of the tree blossomed fair out over the roof of the hall while below stood the trunk within it and the said tree did men call Branstock." When we remember that that name Branstock is the equivalent of Burning Bush we are brought to the very heart of the symbol.

Even today in Germany—and I have seen it also in Switzerland—whenever a new house is built a living tree or a green branch is set up upon the beams at a certain stage as an act of ritual and dedication, creating a world axis in little, a metaphorical Branstock.

Coming to our own tradition, we can think of the cross as the world tree par excellence. There is an old belief, part of our Christian mythology, that the wood from the cross on which Christ was hanged was hewn from one of the trees that grew in Paradise. For Genesis makes a distinction between two world trees—one of the knowledge of good and evil and the other the tree of life. But both trees are specifically said to be in the midst of the garden, therefore at the navel of the earth and one is tempted to ask, with Ananda Coomaraswamy, "whether those trees are not in reality one, a Tree of Life for those who do not eat of its fruits and a Tree of Life-and-Death for those who do." It is a question to be pondered on.

In the Avestan tradition, the ancient writing of the Parsees, usually attributed to Zoroaster, there is also mention of two trees, the Tree of the Solar Eagle, which sprang up from the midst of the ocean on the first day, and the Tree of All Seeds, which grew beside it, of which "the seeds, sent down with the rain, are the germs of all living things."

In every country where the tradition is localized the World Tree is held to be of a species indigenous to that country—for Dante it is an apple, in Siberia a birch, and in Scandinavia an oak tree. For Buddhists it is the Bo tree under which the Buddha was sitting when he received his enlightenment. And in fairy tale, which is, one might say, the myth in little, the myth adapted to the fireside, we have the world tree, nothing less, in the story of Jack and the Beanstalk.

There is no tradition in which the tree in some form or other cannot be found. Think of the design of the Kabbalah, the book par excellence of Jewish mysticism, where the symbolical tree of the Sephiroth is shown as a diagram—even, one might say, the backbone—of the cosmos. Indeed, the tree is clearly to be found in the physical makeup of man himself: the great supporting branch of the spinal column, the trellis of bones, where, according to both Hindu and Chinese tradition, the vital forces move up and down like the ascending and descending angels in that other paradigm of the tree that we know as Jacob's ladder.

But there is another powerful aspect of this all-pervading symbol—one less generally known but ranging through many myths and legends—and that is the inverted tree. There are hints of it in Finland and also in Scandinavia, and there is, as well, an Icelandic riddle that asks, "Hast heard where the tree grows of which the crown is on earth and roots arise in the Heavens?" An Islamic slab in the Byzantine museum at Athens is said to represent an inverted tree supported by two lions. But it is in the earliest writings of Hinduism that one finds it most vividly portrayed, the mysterious Asvattha Tree of the Rig Veda, with its roots in Heaven and its branches spreading downward. Clearly, this tree has a solar aspect, not so much of a physical as of a supernal sun whose rays strike downward, bringing life. Thinking of this most profound of symbols, one remembers Plato's description of man: "Man," he says, "is a heavenly plant; and what this means is that man is like an inverted tree, of which the roots tend Heavenward and the branches downward to earth." And as one symbol invariably leads to another, this in turn reminds us of the Hanged Man of the Tarot cards, who is shown hanging by one foot from the bough of a tree as he swings head downward through the air, his face turned earthward, serene and joyous. And all these can be assimilated to Gurdjieff's system, whose great symbol, the Ray of Creation, is also an inverted tree, rooted above in the Absolute and descending as an octave through ever denser stages of being from one *Do* to another. Clearly the message of this many-faceted symbol is that the roots of man are not on earth but in Heaven and his meaning is that of the Prodigal Son, who, once he arrives at the lowest level, must, if he is to save his life, arise and go to his Father.

Thus do the symbols endlessly repeat themselves, or perhaps it would be truer to say that the one and self-same symbol gives off a light in every direction, just as myths appear in different guises in many times and places. But I think we have to remember that though myth and symbol are an integral part of the traditions, bound up with them, inextricably woven with them, the traditions are not merely myth and symbol. They exist in their own right. They have resisted and continue to resist all our modern attempts to relieve ourselves of responsibility by turning them into fiction. They are so constituted, so replete with meaning that, do what we will—deny, depreciate, or ignore them—we cannot thrust them out of existence. Nor do they need to be restated, no matter how we ourselves may change. They are part of that wisdom which is, as Saint Augustine put it, "Wisdom uncreate, the same now as it ever was and ever will be." And their purpose remains what it has always been—to relate the unknowable to the known and to speak in all their varying tongues the unnameable name from the burning bush. They are here to declare to us the truth, never put better than in the words of the old Greek poet Aratus: "Full of Zeus are the cities, full of Zeus are the harbors, full of Zeus are all the ways of men."

Transcription of a talk given by P. L. Travers for
The Far West Institute, Summer, 1973
Originally published in *Sacred Tradition and Present Need,*
Jacob Needleman and Dennis Lewis, eds. (Viking, 1975)
Reprinted by permission of the Estate of P. L. Travers

THE FAIRY-TALE AS TEACHER

T HE WORD "fairy-tale," because it has so often been misused, is
nowadays a little misleading. Yet it is impossible to dispense with
it or to think of a better. For one thing it is an irrevocable part of our
tradition and, for another, so inclusive. On fairy-tale's broad hearth there
is room for all her children—myth, folk tale, legend, saga—to say nothing of her mighty old pythoness of a mother, religion. This is a
formidable family and it may be that the lapse of the fairy-tale in modern life is due to the fact that nobody wants to face up to such a bunch
of Fates. I have heard parents declare that they did not want their children to read fairy-tales for fear they should grow up into wishful
thinkers. Perhaps in a more candid moment they might rather have said
that they felt inadequate to bring up children who were free to devour
what is, in essence, dynamite. Not that the fairy-tale can hurt anyone;
but it can set up a chain of questions that will only take truth for an
answer. One can hardly imagine a process less encouraging to wishful
thinking!

It would be foolish to deny that the fairy-tale is, indeed, a diversion
for the young. But diversion is only half of it. The other half is concerned with the nature of the world and man's relation to it. In these
matters no one of us is too old to be involved. Fairy-tale is at once the
pattern of man and then chart for his journey. Each of the stories
unwinds from its core the navel-string of an eternal idea. Choose at
random from the simple, most familiar bed-time tales, say, *Hansel and*

Gretel. How it beguiles the child with its lollipop house and the peppermint doorstep! For *us,* however, this is only the lure. The trap, the real secret, is the journey through the wood. If you want to find your way home, it says (back to beginnings, becoming as little children), you must scatter something less ephemeral than peas or rose-leaves. Birds will eat one, and the wind blow the other away. Only by marking the path with pebbles—enduring, hardly found, indestructible—can you pick up the trail and escape the witch's oven which is extinction.

Take *One-Eye, Two-Eyes and Three-Eyes.* Their mother loved One-Eye and Three-Eyes—they were so unique and rare. Two-Eyes was just like everyone else, so she had to fend for herself. Yet it was for Two-Eyes that the fairy feast was spread; Two-Eyes who alone could pluck the gold-and-silver fruit, and Two-Eyes also, whom the Prince so conventionally fancied. Away with oddity cries the story's inner voice. Subhuman and superhuman are both monstrosities. Only the completely normal has a chance to escape the daily bondage and eat the spirit's food.

And what of the *Sleeping Beauty?* Was it wishful thinking, do you think, that broke the spell at last? The story wraps, as in a silk cocoon, an austere admonition. Man, it reminds us, must set a part of himself aside constantly to watch, to cut through the automatically growing forest of his habitual nature so that again and again it may wake the sleeping part. But more than one seed is loosened when you shake the stem of this flowery story. First, eternal vigilance; next, the insistence that Love alone can cut through the tangled thicket; thirdly, it suggests that, while Beauty is the heroine, the Wicked Godmother is the chief character. If she had not waved her wand and cried "Sleep!", how could the arduous business of waking have been set in motion? Hidden things, in ancient writings, are often manifest by means of their opposites; and here the story seems to hint that devils, as well as angels, bless us; that enemies may be useful as friends.

This is only one of the many fairy-tale warnings against sleep. Wizards doze, while their old mothers pluck the three golden hairs that are all their store of wisdom. Giants lie down and sleep and their hearts are stolen away. While the hare takes his siesta, the tortoise wins the race.

The two elder brothers snore at the crossroads while the youngest passes them by and arrives first at the king's palace.

The theme of these Three Brothers bound on a single quest continually recurs. Taken literally, they can be considered as separate entities—Prince Tom, Prince Dick, and Prince Harry. But they can also be regarded as a triple whole, a composite picture of man's inner self. As the first brother, he lives solely by instinct; in the second stage he feels the need for something more but cannot find his direction; only the third brother grown young in acceptance and submission, unashamed to cry Help! to the humblest creature, can claim the bright Princess. The fairy-tales are like water-flowers; they lie so lightly on the surface, but their roots go down deep into a dark and ancient past. They are, in fact, a remnant of that Orphic art whose function it was to instruct the generations in the inner meanings of things. They were not intended to be literature, as such, though the fact that they have, as a by-product, a high literary value is an indication of their Orphic origin. They are a natural growth, not so much inventions as extensions of general experience; objective statements in words as the Sphinx, for instance, is an objective statement in stone. And it must be remembered that they were intended for the ear rather than the eye of the listeners. Listening is the first lesson to be learned from the fairy-tales, as it is from religion—listening that is attention, and inner watching and remembering. While they were still communicated by word of mouth, they came down the generations without distortion. Nowadays it is the reading public that is responsible for the garbled versions. For the eye is less dependable than the ear; it has not the gift of echoes. Those who have heard the fairy-tales have a very different understanding of what they hear from those who have only read them. As a child listens, the story goes in simply as a story. But there is an ear behind the ear which conserves meaning and gives it out much later. It is then that the listener, if he is lucky, understands the nature of the dragon, the necessity for the hero's labors and *who* it is that lives happily ever after.

Luck is an important element in the tales, but they have no truck with wishing. Without luck, you could push a rich man through the eye of a needle sooner than measure up to their requirements. The price of an eye which Odin willingly paid to Mimir in return for the gifts of memory and premonition, was a cut price. He got a bargain and he knew it. In that world nothing is given for nothing and wishing takes you nowhere. Look what happened to Dame Isobel when she became involved with the Flounder![1] There is no easy way out in the fairy-tale. The characters must jump through every hoop. Princes are sent not merely to the end of the world but beyond. But how is that achieved? When you have got to the end of the world what beyond is there? Inwards, answers the hero as he turns in his tracks. Only in this direction can he continue his quest. And that he must do for a traditional fairy-tale term—for ever and a day. Here, as with beyond, it is the day that contains the secret. For ever is time. But the day is Time turning upon itself; it is every moment, the Now that goes in and out with breath, the ultimate ever—Eternity. Not once, and good riddance, must the dragon be slain, but always, second by second. One can think of easier ways of thinking in wishes!

Again, like flowers, the same fairy-tales spring up in different countries, always with the lineaments of first cousins and always alongside the parables of truth that make the religions of man. Like village schoolmasters, they instruct the simple, while the high priests deal with the scholars. But essentially both are concerned with the same teaching. How to live and how to die is the subject of Orphic art, no matter what guises it wears. In effect, this is a single process, for to learn one is to understand the other. And this ancient knowledge, if we but realized it, is continually available. Under all things it lies, the foundation of wisdom. It is as though somewhere in the universe there were a steady lighthouse, a bright wheel turning, whose spokes of light fall now here, now there upon the troubled seas. George Chapman (Homer's Chapman)[2] might well have imagined a similar cosmic phenomenon, such a limitless light-giver, when he wrote:

> *Terror of darkness! O thou king of flames*
> *That with thy music-footed horse dost strike*
> *The clear light out of crystal on dark earth,*
> *And hurl'st instructive fire about the world.*

Instructive fire! This, surely, this effluent and ceaseless light, is what man hankers for when he thinks of the Golden Age. Not lost time perfected, not Eden silted over, but this old knowledge that knocks at his inner ear and makes him long for something he does not know he knows. Hurled about the world we can see its action over the centuries and where it fell upon good ground. This fire was Lao Tse's candle. By its light he formulated his Wordless Doctrine which can never really be told, any more than Buddha's Flower Sermon. Fairy-tale took him too, by the hand, forestalling him, as he was about to die, by setting him on a buffalo and taking him off to Heaven. There he goes, the Old One, forever riding up the sky on his rugged steed; reposeful, neither surprised nor pleased; and ceremoniously bowing, perhaps to Elijah on his cloud.

Again, in India, a fire-bolt fell and brought to light the Vedas, the Upanishads, the Buddhist legends, the Panchatantra stories, and that great well-spring of fairy-tales, the confluence of the *Ramayana* and the *Mahabharata*. This latter pair tell the truths with minstrel voices, decking them out in the most sylvan beauty. Animals and men are complete entities; the forests themselves are living beings. In all fairy-tale where will you find such a figure as Hanuman, such an apotheosis of simplicity and self-surrender as that noble monkey in his role of servant to Rama (Vishnu)? Only the instructive fire could have bracketed so significantly the impulsive ape and the eternal preserver.

In Krishna and the Pandav brothers—silver-helmed Arjuna and tiger-waisted Bhima (Tiger-waisted! Homer had nothing better!) the fairy-tale concentrates the essence of the *Mahabharata*. But the lesser jewels are almost as beautiful—Nala and Damayanti, for instance, and Savitri and Satyavana. Here, in these Indian legends, we find the source that eventually fed the springs of all the Märchen[3] of Europe, Scandinavia and Russia. But we are not to be blamed for knowing so little of our fairy-tale origins; for it is not for much more than a hundred years that the West has had general direct access to the wisdom of the East and the Near East. Did Jakob and Wilhelm Grimm realize, I wonder, that every one of their legendary princes has as his hidden name Rama or Arjuna? Or that Ahmed and Mustapha from *The Arabian Nights* mingle their dark locks with the flaxen curls of Western heroes? For the Thousand and One also derived their heritage from India, though only in part. The other branch of the family came from Persia. There, the instructive fire fell upon the Sufi poets. In the *Mathnawi* of Jalau'uddin Rumi, a brimming cup of parable and story, you may find many a brotherly likeness to the tales of Scheherezade and those we tell our own children at bed-time.

Inevitably, if we go looking for roots, the tracks lead eastwards. The sun of wisdom, like the sun of light, has its rising there. But luckily for us the movement of both is in a westerly direction. As they journey westwards, they adapt the riches they bring with them to each place and age. In the largest sense, therefore, we too have our fairy-tales and allegories and parables that are peculiarly our own. The American Indians have a mine of legend so profuse and varied that it will take generations to collect and digest it. Bunyan's *Pilgrim's Progress* comes into my category—not for the story only but also for the grand simplicity of the writing. The architecture and resonance of the telling are an intrinsic part of the allegory. And think of Blake and his Arabesque inventions—angels, demons, children on clouds, and all the world of spirits. The whole body of his work is fairy-tale, a strong, pliant net set by a cunning fowler to catch the truth.

And still, though we heed it less and less, the wheel turns and the light falls. Never was the instructive fire more needed than it is today. And, as though need, by some universal law, brought forth its own fulfillment, we have a portion of the instructive fire at hand. *All and Everything*[4] by G.I. Gurdjieff seems to me to come under that heading, since its object is to tell man, by means of fairy-tale, parable—call it what you will—the truth about himself. Perhaps I should say re-tell, for it gathers up from the past stray strands of knowledge and plaits them into a powerful web of contemporary exposition. This is a strange, exciting, disturbing book, unique of its kind; occasionally shot through with poetry, continually provocative; alive as a live wire is alive and capable of giving shocks of a very high voltage. Properly to experience it, one must go to it naked, shorn of all preconceived notions of what a book should be. It is a new sort of book. Its difference from other books is in kind, not degree, in the same sense as a camel is different from an ostrich.

Intimately relating opposites to one another (as the fairy-tale never fails to do), this story purports to be told by Beelzebub to his grandson Hassein, a child of twelve years, as they sail through the universe from planet to planet. And the subject of his discourse is the race of "three-brained beings" who inhabit the planet earth. Seated in their spaceship, the storyteller, the child, and their old servant—the intellectual, emotional, and instinctive centers—brood like three Fates upon the race of men. The contrast between the moving ship—a new version of the magic carpet?—and the stillness of those three figures is effectively achieved and very moving. Motionless, wrapped in their tails, their horned heads bowed upon their palms, they seem to gaze with impersonal pity upon the creatures of earth. Here is a fairy-tale for our own time, a piece of objective writing that we cannot read without in some sense experiencing it. The symbolism is accessible to anyone who really wants to understand it and if there are no palpable dragons, there are invisible terrors enough to set the doughtiest hero trembling.

Properly to appreciate this story, one must first hear it read aloud. Only so, I found, can one clarify for oneself the involved rhythms of the writing, and catch, behind the deliberately invented nouns and verbs, their inner meaning ringing. It is necessary, too, for the understanding of the book—the Zen stories make the same demand—to jettison the usual interpretations of certain words and phrases. Anyone used to thinking and feeling in clichés will get nowhere unless he throws over his accumulated ballast. Such words as Consciousness, Self-Consciousness, Reason, Hope, Work, Love—all have to be re-learned in order to understand Beelzebub. Come to that, Beelzebub himself has to be plucked out of his accustomed context. We must here, in effect, give the Devil his due. As for the new words, so full of portent and content, the only way to deal with them is to take them in as children take in grown-up words they do not understand. These act as grains of sand round which the pearl of feeling grows. Without analysis or interpretation, children let a story become part of them and themselves part of it.

The fact that *All and Everything* is told to a child seems to me a hint from the author along the lines of all fairy-tale clues—that the door into the story can only be unlocked by the same key as opens the Kingdom of Heaven. Through Hassein, the grave child, the unfaltering listener, half-grown creature full of the passionate compassion of youth and containing in himself the fructive seed of wisdom, the reader is enabled to look upon himself as in a mirror. In spite of all the poetry, the invention and the flashes of comedy, it is not a pretty picture. Cosmically, man is made to appear at once smaller and larger than he has hitherto conceived himself to be: smaller, because he no longer stands at the center of creation, as the flung stone from which the universe widens ring on ring; larger, because, (though there is a catch in it) he still has, in spite of all he has wasted, the possibility of change. The past may be redeemed and a nobler future prepared. But this possibility—here is the catch—must be used now, worked for at this moment: not after luncheon or tomorrow, but Now. Do you catch the fairy-tale echo?

The cosmology of the book is tremendous. We are shown, as from a height, the worlds harmoniously rising from, or descending into, each other like notes in a universal octave. The cosmic law of Three and Seven are unfolded, recalling us again to the Three Brothers and Seven Brothers of the fairy-tales. Great images abound; the reciprocal feeding of all created things, for instance—which seems miraculous until one realizes it must be true and therefore inevitable. Everything at every moment partakes of something else. What we eat and what we are eaten by is the subject of a large part of the story. The ancients instructed man in his inter-relation with the planets. Paracelsus gave the same reminder when he said we are stars with our bread. And this book repeats the message—with one proviso. That proviso is the core and crux (coeur et Croix would be truer) of Beelzebub's discourse, as it is the underlying implication of all fairy-tales. It is that man must work. His bread he may get by physical sweat; but to eat of the substance of Arcturus and Orion—or nearer home, Jupiter and Venus—he must perform other and harder labors. The provisions for these are explicitly set down in the story. Man must *be* at every second. He must live his life as though it were his death; not turning from the world but, on the contrary, living in the world *alive*. Not just breathing in and out and the years passing.

All and everything the book offers. The fairy-tale word for it was Happy-Ever-After. No fairy-tale, however, ever failed to send in a bill and neither does Beelzebub. In return for all and everything, nothing short of all and everything is demanded. Existence, we are warned, is something that has to be paid for (the plea "I never asked to be born!" would get short shrift here) and time is running out. Dream on, cries the tale, at your peril!

Are we all, then, sleeping beauties, hidden in forests of habit? If shame shakes us and we are honest, the answer must be Yes. Would the earth be where it is if we were not asleep? But there are other atom bombs to be discovered than those that ruin and kill. Every fairy-tale from the beginning of time has been a small explosion, full of healing if man would be healed. The great truths are still to be heard, if man wills to listen, for it is not in his power to silence them. They are objective and outside him.

Many such thunderbolts, many bombs of warning and healing are to be found in this allegory of *All and Everything*. Each chapter throws a new light upon man's condition. The one on America, almost the longest, is also one of the most significant. For it was in America, even though he arraigns it, that Beelzebub found more of that "brotherliness" necessary for man's happier life than in any other country visited. The whole book is, in fact, a brotherly pronouncement. It is as though an elder brother—or, according to the fairy-tale that youngest brother—out of his own deep experience were noting down for us the wisdom he had learned. Reading it is like being wrought upon by a great winnowing fan. One is caught up, small, shamed and shaken, dizzily turning in the air, not knowing whether one will drop among the chaff or the grain. But a large calm falls on the story in the end as the grandson, ever compassionate, asks of his grandfather some comfort for the beings of earth. The answer comes swiftly, cold and bitter, but it lifts up on the wings of poetry because it is true and because it springs from love. And it seems, as we close the book that there is a stir in the enchanted castle and a falling back of those embracing thorns. Stepping through them, the grave child Hassein comes and, lightly touching each upon the shoulder, summons us with the oldest of fairy-tale admonitions— Awake, sleeper, awake!

NOTES

1. An enchanted prince who has the form of a flounder, on being spared by the fisherman, promises him anything he wishes. The foolish fisherman shares this offer with his greedy wife. Again and again she sends him back to the flounder with her demands, first for a nice cottage instead of a hovel, then for a castle instead of a cottage, then she asks to be king, then emperor, and so on until she asks for the power that belongs to God alone. There is then a terrible tempest, and the fisherman and his wife find themselves back where they started, in their pitiful hovel. (Grimm)

2. George Chapman (1559–1634), Elizabethan poet and the translator of Homer referred to in John Keats' sonnet "On First Looking into Chapman's Homer."

3. German word meaning "folk-tales"

4. *Beelzebub's Tales to His Grandson: An Objectively Impartial Criticism of the Life of Man (All and Everything: First Series)* New York: Harcourt, Brace and Company, 1950.

First published in *World Review,* July 1950

Reprinted by permission of the Estate of P. L. Travers

AFTERWORD

Pamela Travers from A to Z

by Jenny Koralek

A is for An Author of Antipodean Ancestry who was convinced that the best poems are written by that essential Anonymity, Anon; and for AE, the Irish mystic, poet, and artist who taught her that the Earth is a living being, and who, after her beloved father, was perhaps the first of many brilliant and exceptional men who "took her by the hand" to guide and inspire her; and for the Answers she never would give; and for the Acceptance she battled for day after day when she was already over ninety, because until then she had never thought of herself as old.

B is for Beyond words, that place she knew how to take us to, by way of what happened in Between, and for her Brooding, the Brooding of a lifetime which started at the edge of the Australian Bush where, as a little girl, she played at being a nesting hen.

C is for the Crack (those mysterious gaps between the first and last strokes of midnight, between the Old Year and the New) where what happens in Between happens; and for the Cauldron of Celtic myth into which she urged us to drop all experiences of joy and sorrow for heat and time to do their transmuting work; and for Communing,

211

those long silent Conversations she so deeply believed contained so much more than Chat or Chatter; and for her treasured, lively, enriching Childhood.

D is for her exhortation to "Dance, dance, wherever you may be," to join that Grand Chain of existence, the linking of Above with Below, which occurs again and again wherever Mary Poppins makes magic and in all her other writings; and for the Dreaming of the aboriginal people of her native land, of that "objective Now" where time stops, that non-moment of wakefulness, the everlasting non-existence from which existence rises.

E is for Eggs, the imaginary ones she laid and tried to hatch as a child long before she discovered the golden Cosmic Egg of Hindu tradition "floating upon the primal waters from which Prajapati, the god of creation will come"; and for the ostrich egg she pondered with her friend, Laurens van der Post—and what it means to the Bushman and to Greek Orthodox Christians.

F is for the Furnished Mind which she most certainly had and much deplored the absence of in others; a mind furnished with the essentials of poetry, the classics, the Bible and nursery rhymes, Shakespeare and riddle-me-rees, folklore, legend, and myth—but no novels, except, perhaps, E.M. Forster's. All her life she worked to bring to life for others the completeness of his famous epigram in *Howard's End:* "It did not seem so difficult. She need trouble him with no gift of her own. She would only point out the salvation that was latent in his own soul, and in the soul of every man. Only connect! That was the whole of her sermon. Only connect the prose and the passion, and both will be exalted and human love will be seen at its highest. Live in fragments no longer. Only connect and the beast and the monk, robbed of the isolation that is life to either, will die."

G is for the Great Goddess, aspects of whom informed her work long before doing so became fashionable; and for her Grasp of the Greening of things as long as stories are told and Games are played, for as long as the "Growing point is Green," all is not lost; and for the Green of her own Growing point when at eighty-two she started on a new *Mary Poppins* book.

212

H is for the Hero or Heroine whose very Humanity, she felt, with its failings and triumphs, serves the true purpose of their existence; and for Happy Ever After, that place she believed exists beyond the opposites we must pass through: "East of the sun and West of the moon, where the fox and the hare say 'goodnight' to each other," not to be confused with Happiness which comes and goes like sunshine and showers.

I is for the Idea she looked for all her life and sometimes felt she was near, and for the Imagination she felt to be "the most essential part of any body's equipment."

J is for the Jerusalem of Psalm 137 ["If I forget thee, O Jerusalem, let my right hand forget her cunning . . . let my tongue cleave to the roof of my mouth if I prefer not Jerusalem above my chief joy . . ."] which represented for her the true center from which we always stray, but "which nevertheless is there" always, within us; and for Joy, the pure anonymous joy when worker and work come together, "with the knowledge that it was not 'I' who did it, but that 'it has been done' . . . "

K is for the flying of Kites; and for the Knowing that must be sacrificed if anything is in fact to be Known; and for the Knights that still and always walk the land, obeying the challenge of the quest, slaying inner dragons, rescuing inner princesses, seeking transformation with their burning question, "Who then am I?"

L is for the Lioness of her birth sign: proud, independent, fiercely protective of her work and her integrity; and for Linking long thoughts; and for Listening, "Sitting inside yourself, very quiet and your ear to the ground"—conditions she considered fundamental for the writer.

M is for the Magic "which happens every day"; and for Much ("In my experience it is always better to have too Much of a thing: too Much can be whittled down and pruned and worked into shape; too little cannot always be increased"); and for Myths, the very embodiment of Meaning which must be "stood under" in silence if they are to be "understood."

N is for the Nursery rhymes she considered the shortest short stories in the world, carrying the origins of all novels, all dramas; and for

Not writing for children, "for who knows where childhood ends and adulthood begins . . . I write to please myself"; and for that No-thing-ness which can only be achieved when the fact is experienced that emptiness is fullness, and fullness emptiness.

O is for the Opposites which appear everywhere in her work and which she understood we must "dance with"; and for her Old age, when she realized that she was not the only one to receive intimations of mystery and meaning, that she had not been singled out, that whatever gifts come from the numinous are received by all men and women, that the picture she had had of herself as ancient crone passing on wisdom had vanished, leaving her suffering, not only her forgetfulness, but the knowledge that she did not know the answers.

P is for Pondering, the "keeping of all sayings and pondering them in her heart," that Patient, tender holding and weighing of thought she learned from Orage (to whom she also owed the contentious notion that one's personal life is no one else's business).

Q is for the Questions for which there are no answers but only more questioning, "fallible creatures that we are"; and for her the realization that "being ourselves in question, we inevitably demand answers to ease the lack within us . . ."

R is for Reconciliation, a major theme in all her work: "Can one set out on the road to Heaven without taking note of the earth one treads on, that lifts the foot forward, giving it wings? How could Purusha make itself known without Prakriti to manifest it? The Self perform its hero tasks without the Ego to contend with? Spirit exhale its vital breath without Body to receive it? Both ends of the stick are necessary."

S is for Sadness and Sorrow, which she did not consider synonymous. (Sadness she considered could not be analyzed, only sensed as a kind of unsatisfactory satiation, of having at the same time too much and not enough, a quintessential lack or loss even at the height of joy: Even as the cup runneth over, the Search continues. Sorrow, on the other hand, underpinned her writing soul "like a heartbeat" behind everything she had written, "life-giving . . . capable of receiving light,

able even to engender it and thereby, through suffering, to be trans-
muted into heart's ease and refreshment"; and for Study, to be kept
by her "always, in my bath, with friends, alone. In this way something comes every day from somewhere . . ."; and for the Star on
her Street, "Yes, right on it!"; and the Secret she shared with many
who said good-bye to her on the doorstep of her house, sending
some in search of it, but mostly without success.

T is for "Three, Three, the Rivals," that universal Triad of interacting
forces which "runs like a bright thread through the true history of
the world, from what is highest to what is"; and for her Tenacity, for
the Twenty years it took her to discover the origins of the tale of
the Ugly Duckling after she heard it was to be found somewhere in
the many volumes of Rumi's *Mathnawi,* and which she celebrated
the finding of with a glass of armagnac; and for her special Talent
for discerning Things not to be spoken of and making it possible for
us to remain a long time silent in front of them.

U is for Unknowing "which is not ignorance. Rather, one could say, a
particular process of cognition that has little or no use for words,"
which "needs that a man be in a certain state of grace, playful, art-
less, inwardly acquitted of opinion . . . rather as fools or saints . . .
which will take us down to the very deeps of knowing . . . cours-
ing through the whole body, artery and vein, provided one can thrust
aside what the world calls common sense, that popular lumpen wisdom that prevents the emerging of the numinous."

V is for the Villains who "awoke the Virtues" . . . those Black Sheep,
who keep things moving along: Jacob who stole his brother's
birthright and Peter Rabbit who stole Mr. MacGregor's lettuces,
Rumpelstiltskin and the Wicked Fairy, the ones who "by strictly
throwing the story forward, bring it to its strict end . . ."; and for
Virtue, whose shared etymology with "Hero" confirmed her view
that each of us is endowed with the possibility to fulfill our promise.

W is for that "deep Well of nothingness, from which poetry, myth and
fairy tales also come, a Well that, no matter how much you take out
of it, is always full to the brim."

X is for "no special word unless you can count xylophone. But nevertheless, it is very important, for what do you put at the end of a letter? X for a kiss, of course."

Y is for Yin and Yang, the Chinese symbol of the "opposites reconciled to themselves and to each other within the encompassing circle."

Z is for Zen, which she studied long and deeply, finding it akin to her own kinds of koan, her many questions put, knowing they would hang in the air long after she had gone; and for Zeus: "Full of Zeus are the cities, full of Zeus are the harbors, full of Zeus are all the ways of men," she loved to quote from Aratus, the ancient pre-Homerian poet, as another expression of her passionate conviction that "if we could only connect" with it, the Godhead is only a hairsbreadth away at any moment.

CONTRIBUTORS

ROB BAKER (1943–1999) died in Fez, Morocco, as this book was going to press, victim of accidental carbon monoxide poisoning. He was executive editor of *Parabola* Magazine from 1979–1980 and co-editor 1987-1992. He was the author of *The Art of AIDS: From Stigma to Conscience* (Continuum, 1994), and *Planning Memorial Celebrations: A Sourcebook* (Bell Tower, 1999). He co-edited *Merton & Sufism: The Untold Story* (Fons Vitae, 1999). At the time of his death, he was completing research on a guide to sacred music of the world.

JONATHAN COTT is a contributing editor at *Parabola* and *Rolling Stone* magazines. A prolific writer, his books include *Pipers at the Gates of Dawn: The Wisdom of Children's Literature* (1983), *Isis and Osiris: Exploring the Goddess Myth* (Doubleday, 1994), *Skies in Blossom: The Nature Poetry of Emily Dickinson* (1995), *Thirteen: A Journey into the Number* (Doubleday, 1996), *Wandering Ghost: The Odyssey of Lafcadio Hearn* (Knopf, 1991), *Search for Omm Sety: A Story of Eternal Love* (Warner, 1989). He has also edited many collections, including *Beyond the Looking Glass: Extraordinary Works of Fairy Tale and Fantasy* (Penguin, 1988), and Volumes 3 and 7 of the *Masterworks of Children's Literature* series.

ELLEN DOOLING DRAPER is the President and co-founder of Living Treasures, Inc., a not-for-profit educational institution which presents public programs celebrating the oral traditions within American culture. Programs have included "The Spirit of New York" (1996), "Our Stories" (1997), "First Contact with The Korubo of the Brazilian Amazon" and "Walking with Creation: Native American Stories of the Beginning and Today" (1998). Daughter of D. M. Dooling, founder of *Parabola, The Magazine of Myth and Tradition,* she served as co-editor from 1988 to 1995, during which time she contributed articles, story retellings, and reviews. She knew P. L. Travers for more than twenty-five years.

JAMES GEORGE, a Rhodes Scholar and Canadian diplomat from Toronto, served as Ambassador/High Commissioner in India, Nepal, Sri Lanka, Iran and the Gulf States. Since his retirement, he has co-founded the Threshold Foundation and the Sadat Peace Foundation, and has been actively engaged in ecological issues. He is a member of the International Advisory Council of the State of the World Forum in San Francisco, and has written numerous articles for *Parabola* and *Resurgence* magazines. His latest book is *Asking for the Earth: Waking up to the Spiritual/Ecological Crisis* (Element, 1995).

BEN HAGGARTY has been a pioneering force in the revival of storytelling in Britain since 1981. He is a founding member of "The Company of Storytellers," runs the Crick-Crick Club in London, and has organized many International Storytelling Festivals in London, Scandinavia, and the United States. He has told a great variety of international traditional tales throughout Europe and North America, particularly the East European Wonder Tales, the epic of "Gilgamesh," the pre-Roman mythology of Britain and Ireland, and the "Mahabharata." He currently runs a center for the research and development of traditional storytelling in the border "Marches" between England and Wales. P.L. Travers knew Ben from his birth and by giving him a subscription to the famous "Puffin Childrens'

Book Club" fostered in him an early love of children's literature and bold narrative.

MARTHA TARPEY HEYNEMAN is a poet, storyteller, and author who lives in Rochester, New York. She studied poetry with Muriel Rukeyser and Karl Shapiro and storytelling with Rafe Martin and Laura Simms. She has written many essays and reviews for *Parabola* Magazine. Her book *The Breathing Cathedral: Feeling Our Way Into a Living Cosmos* was published by Sierra Club Books in 1993. She is presently engaged in the study and composition of poetry and history.

ADRIAN HOUSE was Managing Director of the General Publishing Division of William Collins from 1977 to 1984. He first met P.L. Travers as editor there of *The Fox at the Manger*.

TREBBE JOHNSON has explored the worlds of myth and spirit in poetry, film, journalism, and creative non-fiction. Among the awards she has received are the John Masefield Award of the Poetry Society of America, a grant from the Corporation for Public Broadcasting for a documentary on the Navajo-Hopi land dispute, and a Telly Award for "Only One Earth," a video written for the United Nations Environment Program's celebration of Earth Day. Her work has appeared in *Parabola, Boulevard, The Nation, Harper's, Sierra,* and other publications. She is the Director of Vision Arrow, an organization that sponsors spiritual trips into the wilderness.

PAUL JORDAN-SMITH lives in Seattle where he works as an independent folklore scholar and writer. He holds a M.A. degree in Folklore and Mythology from UCLA, and is presently a Ph.D. candidate in that program. His published writings include numerous essays, reviews, and retellings of folk tales in *Parabola* Magazine, and two chapters in *A Way of Working: The Spiritual Dimension of Craft* (PARABOLA Books). With the late D.M. Dooling, he co-edited *I*

Become Part of It: Sacred Dimensions of Native American Life, an anthology of articles and stories. He is presently at work on his doctoral dissertation, *For As Many As Will: Deciphering a Folk Event,* a study of folk dancing, storytelling, and other folk activities.

JENNY KORALEK is an English children's author. She was born in South Africa and raised and educated in England and at the University of Paris, France. She is the author of more than thirty titles including *The Friendly Fox,* Beverley Gooding, illus. (Little, Brown 1988), *The Cobweb Curtain,* Pauline Baynes, illus. (Henry Holt, 1989), *The Boy and the Cloth of Dreams,* James Mayhew, illus. (Candlewick Press, 1994—named best illustrated book by *The New York Times Review of Books,* 1995), *Cat and Kit,* Patricia McCarthy, illus. (Hyperion, 1994), *Once Upon Olympus: an Introduction to the Greek Myths* (Cambridge University Press, 1998), and *Night Ride* (forthcoming in 2000 from Candlewick Press). She was a close friend of P.L. Travers for more than thirty years.

BRIAN SIBLEY is an English writer and broadcaster. His radio drama credits include the BBC's serializations of J.R.R. Tolkien's *The Lord of the Rings,* C.S. Lewis' *The Chronicles of Narnia,* and P.L. Travers' *The Fox at the Manger.* His most recent radio series are *Disney's Women, Ain't No Mickey Mouse Business,* and *A Century of Cinema.* Other works include a musical stage play, *To Sea in a Sieve,* based on the life of Edward Lear, numerous books including *Shadowlands, The Land of Narnia, The Book of Guinness Advertising,* and *The Disney Studio Story* (with Richard Holliss). His most recent books are about the making of *The Wrong Trousers* and *A Close Shave,* Nick Park's Oscar-winning films starring Wallace and Gromit. He worked with P.L. Travers on a so-far unmade movie sequel to Disney's *Mary Poppins.*

LAURENS VAN DER POST (1906–1996), born in South Africa, was an author, anthropologist, philosopher, explorer, and soldier who became mentor to Britain's Prince of Wales and to former Prime Minister Margaret Thatcher. His books included *The Lost World of the Kalahari*

(1958), *The Heart of the Hunter* (1961), *Jung and the Story of Our Time* (1976), *First Catch Your Eland* (1978), *A View of All the Russias* (1964), *Flamingo Feather* (1955), and his last book, *The Admiral's Baby*, was published just after his death.

PHILIP ZALESKI is lecturer in religion at Smith College and senior editor of *Parabola* Magazine. His books include *The Recollected Heart, The Gifts of the Spirit*, and a forthcoming anthology of writings about heaven (with Carol Zaleski). He is the editor of the annual series, *The Best Spiritual Writing*. His writings appear regularly in *The New York Times, First Things, Parabola*, and many other periodicals.

FEENIE ZINER is a writer living in Branford, Connecticut. She was Professor of English at the University of Connecticut from 1974 to 1993, and before that, taught at Sir George Williams University, Montreal, McGill, SUNY Purchase, and The New School for Social Research. Her books include *Cricket Boy* (Doubleday, 1978), *Bluenose, Queen of the Grand Banks* (Nimbus, Halifax, 1980), *Squanto* (Shoe String Press, 1988), *Pilgrims & Plymouth Colony* (American Heritage, 1963), *A Full House* (Simon and Schuster, 1967), *Duck of Billingsgate Market* (Four Winds, 1975), and *Counting Carnival* (Coward McCann, 1965). An autobiographical account of a sojourn in British Columbia called *Within this Wilderness* was published in 1978 by W.W. Norton, and has just been reissued (1999) by A Common Reader. She has also contributed journal articles to *Yale University Press, American Journal of Psychoanalysis*, and *Parabola*, and served as children's book reviewer for the *Montreal Star* and *The New York Times Book Review*. She was a frequent contributor of essays to *Northeast*, published by the *Hartford Courant*.

INDEX

222

Index